# A Guide to
# SCOTLAND'S COUNTRYSIDE

# A Guide to

# SCOTLAND'S COUNTRYSIDE

### Roger Smith

## Macdonald Publishers, Edinburgh

Published by
Macdonald Publishers
Loanhead, Midlothian
EH20 9SY

ISBN 0 86334 054 7

Designed and edited by Margaret Horne

Jacket designed by Michael Bassi
Front jacket photograph: An Teallach, Wester Ross, Highland
(*photograph by David Paterson*)
Back jacket photograph: Invereshie, near Aviemore, Highland
(*photograph courtesy of Scottish Tourist Board*)

*Printed in Scotland by*
Macdonald Printers (Edinburgh) Limited,
Edgefield Road, Loanhead, Midlothian EH20 9SY

# CONTENTS

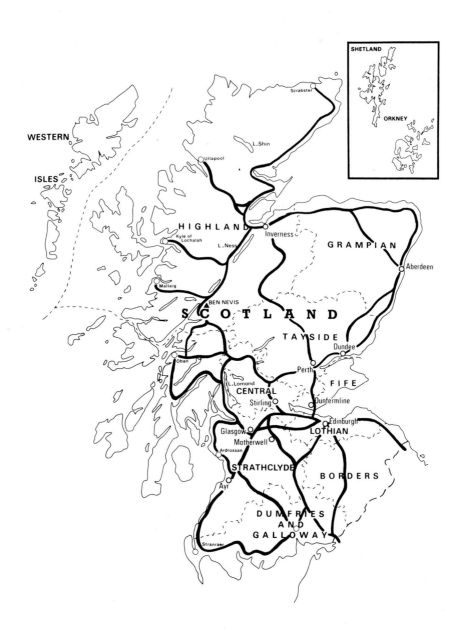

*Map of Scotland, showing major roads*

# FOREWORD

It has been my good fortune to have lived and worked close to Scotland's countryside for much of my life and the beauty of the Scottish hills, lochs, rivers and glens has given me great joy. I know that this joy has also been experienced by countless thousands of people from many parts of the world who have come to know and love Scotland.

Our countryside is becoming increasingly popular as a base for recreation and tourism, as well as being a vital economic resource for those whose livelihood depends upon the land. Whatever form their recreation may take, people do wish to have access to the countryside to enjoy its peace and beauty; but, equally, we all have to understand that access in the wrong place or at the wrong time can cause real problems for farmers with their crops and stock, for foresters with the risks of fire, and for deerstalkers in the autumn. All of these people have to earn their livelihood in the same countryside in which we seek our recreation. Maintaining a balance between the demand for public enjoyment, the conservation of wildlife and scenic beauty, and productive land uses calls for a deep understanding of the long-term needs of both countryside and people. Such an understanding can do much to avert conflict.

This book is more than simply a gazetteer of things to see and do; it also aims to help the reader discover just what it is that we cherish so much in our countryside heritage, and to learn how each one of us can play our part in helping to conserve and care for it, for the benefit of tomorrow's generations as well as today's. The author has gathered a great deal of information from many sources in compiling this guide and, whilst the idea for the book's production was largely inspired by this Commission's earlier publication *Scotland's Countryside*, it is Roger Smith's knowledge – and the sensitive appreciation of the Scottish countryside for which he is well known – that will ensure this new guide enjoys the success it deserves.

David W. Nickson, CBE, DL
*Chairman, Countryside Commission for Scotland*

# ABOUT THIS BOOK

This book is in line of succession from the three editions of the Countryside Commission for Scotland's *Official Guide to Scotland's Countryside*, which was last revised in 1977 to mark the Queen's Jubilee year. Coincidentally, that was the year I came to live and work in Scotland. Whilst not able to undertake another edition themselves, the Commission felt that the basic idea of the *Guide* was worth continuing.

The result is in your hands, and while it owes a great deal to the *Guide* in terms of inspiration and format – a debt I am very happy to acknowledge – it is an entirely new work. I have tried to expand both main sections of the book, while always keeping in mind that its contents should be not only interesting, but informative and useful to the visitor.

It has still been difficult to decide not what to put in, but what to leave out. I realised very quickly after coming to live in Scotland that the range of attractions in its countryside, for the discerning visitor, is staggering. Whether your taste is for romantic ruined castles with long histories of clan warfare, a tour round a distillery to see how 'Scotland's national drink' is produced, or a trip on a steam train, you can find it here.

Besides all this—perhaps I should say above all this—is the countryside itself. The landscape of Scotland is renowned the world over for its beauty and variety, and many pens blessed with an eloquence far greater than mine have written its praises. It is a land which the visitor has, by and large, great freedom to enjoy. This brings responsibilities and a section of this book gives brief details of some of the bodies acting as conservators of our wildlife, our flora and the land itself.

The book is divided into two main sections. The introductory pages attempt to give a broad description of Scotland's countryside – the natural features, the flora and fauna, the industries that use its resources, the sport and recreation that takes place in it, and so on. The main part of the book is a gazetteer of what you can see and do in the countryside in Scotland. It is as complete as we could make it, but it is in the nature of such things to change from time to time, and I would be very grateful if anyone finding an error or an alteration of fact would advise me, via the publishers, so that future editions can be corrected.

Finally, perhaps I should define 'countryside' as used in this book. There are many splendid things to see and do in Scotland's towns and cities, but it is not in my brief to describe them here, and so anything in an urban area has been left out. All such places have excellent guides available for the visitor. Villages are included, however, and where addresses in towns needed to be given (for example, for Area Tourist Boards), this has been done.

Putting this book together has been a tremendously enjoyable task. Sometimes, as the pile of information grew higher, I doubted if it would ever be finished. It is no doubt imperfect, but I hope that it fulfils my aims of being informative and useful, and does indeed help you to get to know Scotland's magnificent countryside.

Roger Smith

*Note:* Any opinions expressed in the text are my own. No responsibility can be accepted for any errors or inaccuracies that may have occurred.

## Acknowledgements

I am grateful to the National Trust for Scotland for granting permission to reproduce the photographs on pages 107, 110 and 157 and to the Scottish Tourist Board for all the other photographs in this book.

# PART I
# AN INTRODUCTION TO
# SCOTLAND'S COUNTRYSIDE

# LANDSCAPE AND GEOLOGY

No visitor to Scotland could fail to be impressed by the grandeur of the scenery. It is the most mountainous part of Britain, with a deeply indented sea coast on the west, superb glens containing fine lochs, a tapestry of wonderful islands and, for contrast, an eastern quilt of fertile farmland edged by a seaboard with splendid cliffs and some of Britain's best and longest beaches.

It is the variety of the scene which impresses most of all, the more so as one gets to know the land a little better. What are the underlying reasons for this variety? In the more dramatic areas, much of the cause dates back to the Ice Ages, when glaciers carved out the glens, high corries and the rock basins which today contain lochs.

In geological terms, Scotland cannot be divided into 'highland' and 'lowland' as easily as the eye might suggest. The underlying rock strata are complicated and require more space than I have here to explain. It is always worth watching what is under your feet as you travel through Scotland: a simple selection of rock types might include basalt from Mull, gabbro from Skye, quartzite from Torridon, gneiss from Sutherland, granite from Cairngorm or Rannoch.

Among Scotland's most obviously dramatic physical features are the 'faults', where massive fractures in the rock strata have occurred in the distant past. One such fault runs along the Highland edge between Helensburgh, on the Firth of Clyde, and Stonehaven, south of Aberdeen; another lies along the line of the Great Glen from Fort William to Inverness.

The visitor standing on the ramparts of Stirling Castle is in the middle of an elementary lesson in geology. To the north-east runs the southern scarp face of the Ochil Hills, the line of another large fault – now only 2,000 feet (600 m) in altitude, but along which the rocks south of the fault have dropped some 10,000 feet (3,050 m). All around Stirling is the Carse, a very flat area of rich farmland through which the River Forth winds in serpentine loops. The Carse and its heavy clay soils formed at a time of higher sea levels, after the Ice Age, making a marine estuary with the sea penetrating far west of Stirling.

Castle Rock itself is a fine example of an igneous intrusion, or volcanic plug, as is Abbey Craig on which Wallace's monument sits, looking for all the world like a Gothic space rocket waiting to take off. The Gargunnock Hills to the south-west are made of a pile of lavas some 350 million years old and further west rise the older Highland rocks.

A brief look at Scotland's geology can start with the areas south of the Forth and Clyde. Glaciation was just as widespread here as it was further north, but here the land was less fretted and gouged, and the effects of the ice are thus generally more subdued. Dramatic features can be found, one of the most accessible being the very fine corrie or hanging valley in which sits Loch Skeen and out of which drops the Grey Mare's Tail waterfall, on the Selkirk to Moffat road. This inspiring scene is appreciated even more by those doing the splendid ridge walk south of the road, from Bodesbeck to Herman's Law.

The ice retreated here to leave a large plateau, with rounded hill forms and gentle river valleys, although there is more cut and thrust about the Galloway landscape to the south-west, with a greater contrast in the hardness of the local rock types. The Southern Uplands contain few notable stretches of water, St Mary's Loch being an exception; man's very recent works in damming and making reservoirs have provided more than nature did herself.

Near Melrose, the Eildon Hills stand out as three knobs of harder material that have worn down less than the surrounding land; they have been a landmark since prehistoric times. To the east, the Berwickshire Merse gives another rich farming plain, and the coast is surprisingly dramatic, with sandstone cliffs reaching several hundred feet out of the North Sea around St Abb's Head and providing a noted sea-bird sanctuary (now a reserve).

The Central Belt, where most of Scotland's population is concentrated and where much of the industry arose, also contains fine detailed glacial features such as *kames* (terraces of debris formed by water flowing between a shrinking glacier and the valley sides), seen at Carstairs and other places. Loch Leven in Fife fills an ice basin, left as the glaciers retreated. I have mentioned the volcanic plugs in and around Stirling: underneath this are many seams of coal – the basis of industrialisation – and mining has been extensively carried out.

The Helensburgh – Stonehaven fault crosses the southern end of Loch Lomond and can be clearly seen by climbing Conic Hill from the car park at Balmaha. The sharp division is apparent here: to the north, all the scenery is recognisably 'highland' in character, whereas to the south it is all lower ground. Loch Lomond itself is a deep rock basin, narrowing at its northern end to Glen Falloch, through which the A82 road and the railway squeeze. The loch is fed by dozens of burns, but its only outlet is the short River Leven.

Travelling north on the A82, one sees an example of the way man has used glaciation in the hydro scheme based on Loch Sloy. The feeder pipes and pumping station are alongside the road at Inveruglas.

North of Loch Lomond, the great extent of high ground known as the Grampian Mountains becomes apparent. If you are able to climb to one of the principal summits, you will see that most of the hills lie at about the same height, and from this viewpoint, though not from below looking up, it is apparent that much of the landscape has evolved through downward erosion. The rainfall is higher in the west, so the river valleys tend to be steeper and more dramatic. Gorges occur, as in the Nevis and

Corrieshalloch. The western Grampians thrust up as a huge mass of granites and lavas, with the dome of Ben Nevis rising above all at 4,409 feet (1,344 m). Frost is less severe generally in the west than in central and eastern areas, where notable examples of frost-shattering occur on the prominent 'tors' on such eastern hills as Beinn a'Bhuird, Ben Avon and Bennachie in Aberdeenshire.

The magnificent sea lochs of western Scotland are glacial troughs drowned by a rise in the sea level. In some places (Lochs Hourn and Nevis, for example), the landscape is reminiscent of Norway's fjords, the lesser height of the hills being the main difference. The smaller scale somehow seems to add an approachability and charm to the Scottish landscape, and makes it less forbidding without losing its grandeur.

In the far north-west, a strip from Glenelg to Loch Eriboll contains some of the most ancient rocks in the land. Massive Torridonian sandstones overlie Lewisian gneiss; sometimes the gneiss outcrops and is dominant, and this very old, hard rock gives the Sutherland landscape its unique character, with hills rising abruptly from a plain of peat studded with hundreds of small lochans. From these rise wonderful isolated hills – Suilven, Ben Stack and Ben More Assynt/Coigach are all fine examples. It is a landscape primitive in its form and moving in its effect on the observer.

A narrow band of limestone gives the cave features such as Smoo and Inchnadamph (and startling green grass around them), and the northern edge of mainland Scotland is noted for its fine rugged cliffs and deep cave-like inlets known as *geos*. Other features of the west and north include raised beaches (Islay, Jura and Mull) and the extraordinary basalt cliffs found on many of the islands. Fingal's Cave on the small island of Staffa is well known and can be visited by boat. It inspired the composer Felix Mendelssohn to write his *Hebridean* overture.

The Cairngorm granite, east of the modern A9 road, has resisted weathering to the extent that it now forms the largest contiguous area over 2,000 feet (600 m) in Britain. It is often referred to as a plateau, but in fact contains magnificent corries on Cairngorm itself, Braeriach and other hills, and a wonderful water feature in Loch Avon, hidden in the hills at an altitude of 2,300 feet (700 m). To the south-east of the main massif is a noted 'frost hollow', as the inhabitants will readily agree, in the village of Braemar. Cold air coming down from the mountains becomes trapped here, the woodlands along the Dee valley further hindering its escape. Frost has been recorded in every month of the year, with the lowest temperature in British meteorological history standing at −27°C to Braemar's credit (if that is the right word).

The lower hills of Aberdeenshire and Buchan run down to the sea in a more regular pattern than the western hills. They are divided by river valleys, some of which are actually diverted passages, where the original channel was cut off by boulder clay deposited by glaciers. The temporary damming and release leads to gorge features, as in the lower Don and the former Dee spillway, north of Ballater.

The east coast has a much simpler form than the west, with few major inlets. It is very fine coastal scenery, nevertheless, with long sandy beaches backed with dunes and fretted cliffs. These features can be seen at Stonehaven (a wonderful little harbour), Peterhead and much further north in Caithness, where the Ord presented a severe problem to communications engineers that was not solved until very recently.

This very brief outline of Scotland's landscape has of course omitted much – the parallel roads of Glen Roy (ancient lake beaches); the machair of the western seaboard of the Hebridean islands; the dramatic coasts of the Orkney and Shetland Islands; the tidal flats of Solway. A lifetime's study of this fascinating subject is not enough; at the end of it, or even after one visit to Scotland, I doubt if you would share the view of James Hogg, writing in 1802:

> There is not a green spot to be seen, and the hill . . . to the westward is still more terrific than any to the south, and is little inferior to any in the famous Glencoe behind it. It is one huge cone of misshapen and ragged rocks, entirely peeled bare of all soil whatever, and all scarred with horrible furrows torn out by the winter torrents.*

He was writing of Buachaille Etive Mor, one of Scotland's most magnificent and best-loved mountains. Times have indeed changed in the way that we appreciate landscape, though, to be fair to Hogg, he did write with a shepherd's eye!

* From *Highland Tours*, reissued in 1981 by Byways Books, Hawick.

# THE FACE OF THE LAND

If we could see one of those enormously speeded-up films, taken from high above Scotland and covering the past 5,000 years, it would show sustained activity somewhere or other pretty well throughout that long period of time. The intensity of the activity would naturally fluctuate, but in general the pattern would be an accelerating one, with the past 150 years shown as a frenzy of building, demolishing and rebuilding both in our towns and in industry.

If the film concentrated on the country areas, the activity would still continue, but at a much slower rate. None the less, there are few parts of Scotland where man has not striven to clear, burn, cultivate, build or dig into for raw materials. We are still altering the face of the land, but our methods nowadays tend to affect much greater areas in a more radical fashion.

Where would the film first show activity? Surprisingly, perhaps, in the Outer Isles or in Orkney and Shetland. Before the film started, there were scattered communities, very small in number, in coastal areas on both west and east sides of the country – the long barrow of Dalladies near Montrose has been dated to about 3400 BC. We start, however, with a genuine community using stone dwellings which can still be seen. Skara Brae in the Orkneys is a remarkable place; the 'houses' contain bed frames, stone shelves and storage boxes. It is believed to have been occupied from about 3000 to 2400 BC. There were similar settlements in Shetland.

Remains of settlements, burial grounds, or places of holy or ritualistic significance from this period and that following it can be found in many parts of Scotland, from Galloway through the Central Belt (for example, Cairnpapple Hill in West Lothian) right up to the magnificence of the Callanish standing stones on Lewis. Any of these venerable monuments to a past civilisation is worth a visit.

From the Roman period, there are few visible remains. Parts of the Antonine Wall can still be seen – there is an excavated section and fort at Bar Hill, Twechar, for instance – but the legions left much less reminder of their power in Scotland than they did further south. After they left, and up to the first period of medieval building, much is still unclear. We have Celtic crosses and carvings, notably in Argyll, but little else apart from the magnificent illustrated manuscripts which are a reminder of the light the early Christians kept burning.

Our activity really starts speeding up in the eleventh and twelfth centuries, with the building of the great religious houses in the Borders – the abbeys at Melrose, Jedburgh, Dryburgh and elsewhere – and the

B

establishment of the first burghs, the forerunners of today's towns. Fortifications and strongholds were important to the landowners of the day, and castles began to become a part of the scene around this time.

These were followed in the Middle Ages by the peculiarly Scottish fortified tower, splendid examples of which can be seen in many different areas. Not surprisingly, the Borders saw plenty of action and have the best collection of towers, fought over and defended for hundreds of years. Such places as Hermitage, Smailholm and Neidpath give an idea of how important it was for the lairds of the time to be able to defend their land in secure houses.

The Borders also offer us the oldest continually inhabited house in Scotland, at Traquair, which has over 500 years of history behind it. Town houses from this period are rare, and country houses even rarer; most of the remaining examples date from the time of 'improvement' of estates in the eighteenth or even nineteenth century.

This was indeed a rich period of change in the countryside. With a more settled political situation, the owners of great estates turned their attention to their houses and land. Many were the fine buildings erected in this period, and the land itself altered quite dramatically in many places. Large areas were planted with trees and the policies of Atholl, Rothiemurchus and others bear witness to this activity today. Experiments in silviculture led to the introduction of species from other lands, as can be seen at such places as Dawyck (near Peebles) and the estate of the Earls of Glasgow at Kelburn, overlooking the Firth of Clyde.

At around this time, industry made its first strong marks on the land, with the setting up of mills in the Tweed Valley, coal mining in Lothian and Fife, and the first distilleries for whisky in the Highlands and Islands. The communications map altered radically, and this is dealt with in more detail in the next section.

Over the past century the activity has continued unceasingly. Towns have spread into the countryside and remote areas have been deliberately chosen for the sites of such places as nuclear power stations and construction yards for large structures connected with the search for oil and gas in our oceans. Power must be taken from where it is generated to where it is consumed, and so we have the march of pylons across the land. Hydro works have appeared in many areas of the Highlands, creating dams, new lochs and demanding access roads.

The activity will not cease and, in the same way that no writer of a century ago could have foreseen our motorways, electricity pylons or oil platform yards, I cannot forecast what we may see in the century ahead. Man cannot, it seems, be still and rest with what he has. He must always be venturing, building, pulling down and changing the face of the land. Scotland could be likened to an old – indeed an ageless – lady whose face, despite the many bumps, scars and lines upon it, is still beautiful. I hope we will have the sense to keep it that way.

# TRANSPORT AND COMMUNICATIONS

The communications map of Scotland is a testament to man's enduring habit of attempting the seemingly impossible, and succeeding despite all. Faced with difficult terrain, hostile weather and opposition from landowners, local people and central government – and sometimes all three – roads, tracks, railways and canals have nevertheless been pushed through. In some cases the eventual destination was not that aspired to at the start of the enterprise, but that has not seemed to matter – the over-riding desire to link two places previously unconjoined has been satisfied.

## Roads

The first lasting marks upon the land were made by the Romans, whose lines of forts extending up through southern Scotland and the lower-lying eastern coastal areas were inevitably joined by roads. Few real traces remain, although Dere Street can be walked from the Border towards Selkirk and the stronghold of Trimontium.

By medieval times, with the granting of burgh charters and the setting up of regular markets, routes for pedlars and traders were well established, particularly in southern and central Scotland. North of Perth the country was largely unexplored by travellers; there were no important markets and the clan system with its many warring factions was another substantial deterrent.

Cross-Scotland routes became more important with the rise in the cattle trade. Drovers from as far away as Skye took their beasts to the 'trysts' at Crieff and Falkirk; from there they were driven on through the borderlands to the English markets – even to London. The drove roads used in the seventeenth and eighteenth centuries can be traced in many places. One ran from Glenelg, which was reached by swimming the beasts across the narrows from Skye, through Glen Garry to the Great Glen and then over the high moorland to Speyside. The route then ran south to Perth and Stirling, before reaching Falkirk. Traces of these drove routes remain in the use of the Gaelic *bo* or *ba* (cattle) in place-names. The hardiness of beast and drover is shown by the example of the *Bealach na Bà* (Pass of the Cattle) in Applecross, another through-route from the north-west; the pass is at well over 2,000 feet (600 m). It is now drivable and is one of the most spectacular roads in all Scotland.

Notable trading routes in eastern Scotland included the Mounth roads linking Deeside and the Angus glens. Jock's Road from Braemar to Glen Doll is today a noted walking route, and others from Ballater to Glen Doll and from Aboyne to Tarfside over Mount Keen (a route used by Queen Victoria) are just as good. Many of these routes are now public rights of way.

The road-building programme led by General George Wade after the 1715 Rising was a major step forward. Garrisons were established or strengthened at Fort William, Fort Augustus, Fort George (near Inverness), Ruthven (near Kingussie), and Bernera by Glenelg, and these were linked by military roads. In only seven years, Wade directed the building of 242 miles (387 km) of road at a total expenditure of £16,000. Thirty bridges were constructed, replacing difficult fords in many cases. The most ambitious undertaking was the Corrieyairack Pass between Fort Augustus and Speyside, reaching 2,500 feet (770 m) at the summit. All these routes had to be negotiable by hauled artillery, and the Corrieyairack has 17 hairpin bends on the upper section. It is a splendid walk today.

Wade's successor, Edward Caulfeild, continued the work after the 1745 Rising had been extinguished at Culloden. Roads were pushed further into the West Highlands, south to Stirling, Dumbarton and Inveraray, and east to Stonehaven and Coupar Angus. The legend 'General Wade's Military Road', which adorns many Ordnance Survey sheets of Scotland, is used rather liberally to include roads built by Caulfeild and others!

In the late eighteenth and early nineteenth centuries, civil engineers turned their attention to Scotland. Roads were built by Mitchell from Fort William to Newtonmore and by Telford from Fort William to Mallaig, Dingwall to Lochcarron, Dingwall to Lairg and Tongue, and the famous route over the Ord of Caithness to link Dornoch, Helmsdale and Wick. This was the first eastern route into Caithness.

By the mid-nineteenth century, the major road network was beginning to take the shape it has today – coaches ran between Edinburgh and Inverness as early as 1820. The route south from Glasgow to Carlisle had been completed by Telford (the modern M74/A74) and the difficult coast route from Edinburgh to Berwick (A1) was also finished. Improved technology in the twentieth century has meant that the demands of the motor traveller and freight companies for fast smooth roads can be met. In 1932 the 'new road' from Bridge of Orchy to Glencoe replaced the one designed by Wade (Wade's road is now part of the West Highland Way long-distance footpath), and more recently motorway construction has stamped a high-speed triangle between Glasgow, Edinburgh and Stirling. Bridges have replaced ferries at such places as Ballachulish, Kessock (Inverness) and notably the Forth and Tay estuaries. The 'new' A9 will shortly be completed, giving a fast route all the way from Glasgow and Edinburgh to Inverness.

Notwithstanding all these improvements, some of the most enjoyable motoring in Scotland is still on the narrow roads of the north and west, and I personally hope that they will be left as they are – it does us all good to slow down once in a while.

*Buachaille Etive Mor, Glencoe, Highland*

# Railways

The terrain of Scotland presented exceptional challenges to the railway engineers, and they responded in an exceptional manner. Railways, particularly the single-track lines, seem to me to fit into the environment better than modern roads, taking up much less ground. Furthermore, Highland railway architecture, such as the Glenfinnan viaduct and the line above Loch Long, can be accepted as an addition to the scenery rather than as an intrusion upon it.

The first lines to be built were naturally those linking the major cities and linking them with the south. By the mid-1850s lines had been built between Edinburgh and Glasgow, and from both cities south into England. The more adventurous and ambitious routes soon followed – the route to Inverness, reaching well over 1,000 feet (300 m) at Drumochter and Slochd, was completed in 1863. Before long thought was being given to the crossing of the Tay and Forth, to take the line from Edinburgh to Dundee and on to Aberdeen. The first Tay Bridge was destroyed in a great gale in December 1879, but its successor still carries trains, as does the Forth Rail Bridge, opened in 1890 on a foul day by the then Prince of Wales. It is reported that the Prince was driven to the new bridge in his carriage, opened the bridge with very few words, and then left without further delay!

The line to Fort William presented great difficulty. The route crosses Rannoch Moor – the only alternative, via Lochs Awe, Etive and Leven, would have been too circuitous and costly. The moor is mostly peat and the line was literally 'floated' on logs and brushwood. It includes, at Corrour, one of Britain's most remote stations. This station was originally provided for the use of sporting estates, and has no road access, but today it is a valuable stopping point for walkers, with Loch Ossian youth hostel (also without public-road access) a mile (1½ km) away.

The west-coast lines to Oban, Mallaig and Kyle of Lochalsh were subsidised by government funds (they were of course built in the days of private railway companies), and were intended to serve remote communities and provide outlets for island trade which never really materialised. The engineering is magnificent throughout, and although these lines could never be profitable and are under constant threat of closure, they make such splendid journeys that to close them would seem a terrible shame. It would surely be better to promote them more vigorously as a major tourist attraction and accept that for some part of the year they must be operated as a public service.

Another splendid run is that from Inverness to Wick, with its long inland detour to Lairg. This line was sponsored by the Duke of Sutherland, who spent over £200,000 of his own money in building it through his vast estates. A plan to extend the line westwards from Lairg to Ullapool was never put into effect.

Many other grandiose and quite unworkable railway plans never saw the light of day, including one for an 'atmospheric' railway along the west coast to include a tunnel right through Ben Nevis! Other lines closed after brief careers and can be walked today, including parts of the Caledonian line from Stirling to Crianlarich and the Waverley route from Edinburgh through the Borders to Carlisle.

# Canals

There have been three major canal-construction projects in Scotland; two of them are still open, but the third – the Forth–Clyde – is largely closed, although some restoration work has taken place in recent years.

The Forth–Clyde canal was the initiative of Sir Lawrence Dundas, who owned land at both ends of the route. Work began in 1768, but there were many engineering and financial problems and it was 1790 before the full length of 35 miles (56 km) was open to traffic. Its sponsor's influence can still be seen in Glasgow, where Port Dundas Road appears on the street maps. The canal's eastern terminus was Grangemouth, and at its peak it carried 3,000 vessels a year.

The Crinan Canal was built to cut out the long passage round the peninsula of Kintyre, a journey much affected by storms. It was engineered by Rennie and was opened in 1801. The canal is still navigable and is used today by pleasure craft and small coasters.

Scotland's major canal project is the Great Glen route from Fort William to Inverness – Telford's Caledonian Canal. It was felt that the route would cut out the Pentland Firth passage, thereby making it easier for Baltic traders to reach the west coast; it would be of military value; and it would also promote the herring fisheries of the Minch and the inner Atlantic. It links Lochs Lochy, Oich and Ness with locked sections and its construction was a major feat of civil engineering. The Caledonian Canal first opened in 1822, but after twenty years had to be closed for major repairs, reopening in 1847. It has largely been superseded as a trade route by better roads, railways and bigger ships which can navigate the northern seas successfully. It is still much used by fishing boats and pleasure craft, making a fine and most unusual journey, and the towpath stretches are enjoyable and interesting walks.

# FORESTRY

In its natural state, Scotland is a land of trees. Over many centuries, man's activities and climatic changes have combined to reduce the tree cover to less than a quarter of what it was in prehistoric times. If you had lived in Scotland 5,000 years ago, you would have found dense forests of oak, hazel, wych elm and alder, with juniper, birch and pine higher up the hills. The tree cover reached about 2,000 feet (600 m) – rather higher than it does today, even in ideal planting conditions.

The first written reference to the Scottish landscape comes from the Roman historian Strabo, who says of the inhabitants, a scattered race living in small settlements, 'Forests are their cities, for having enclosed an ample place with felled trees, they make themselves huts therein and lodge their cattle.'

The Romans made a number of forays into Scotland, building the Antonine Wall from the Forth to the Clyde and establishing forts and outposts as far north as the Moray Firth. As with all Roman colonies, roads were built, and where these crossed difficult ground, logs were laid to give a 'bottoming'. This was probably the first serious inroad by man into the forest of Scotland. Wood was also used for fencing, to make houses and for implements such as crude ploughs.

After the Romans left, climatic changes which are still not fully understood led to considerable areas of the forest dying into the peat and failing to regenerate. Peat cutting and long spells of very dry weather will still expose the massive roots of trees from this period.

In the twelfth and thirteenth centuries, notably in the Borders, large areas were cleared to provide grazing for sheep. The monks of the abbeys at Melrose, Jedburgh, Kelso and elsewhere were great agriculturists and improvers, draining marshes, enclosing arable land, practising crop rotation – and felling trees. It is believed that in the mid-thirteenth century, Melrose Abbey alone ran 12,000 breeding sheep.

The process of felling continued. Cultivation spread along the drier east-coast areas; oak and birch were cut for smelting, oak and pine for the fine timber needed for ships; and later on, considerable felling took place to reduce the available habitat for wolves. The great Caledonian forest was drawn back to the area west and north of the Great Glen. Touring Ross-shire in 1724, Daniel Defoe remarked on 'Woods reaching from ten to fifteen and twenty miles in length . . . rendered of no use merely for want of convenience of water carriage to bring them [felled trees] away'.

Dr Johnson, however, saw differently in 1773. On his famous tour of Scotland, he passed the judgement that 'a tree in Scotland is as rare as a horse in Venice'. But all was not decay and destruction. The great landowners had become interested in planting and restocking trees from the time that John Evelyn published his 'discourse on forest trees' entitled *Sylva*. That was in 1664, and in the ensuing century planting proceeded at a number of great estates. The larch was introduced, notably by the 4th Duke of Atholl, who is credited with planting 10,000 acres (4,050 ha) during his lifetime. Other trees new to the Scottish scene were the Norway spruce and silver fir.

David Douglas, a great naturalist and plant collector, visited America at the request of the Horticultural Society of London and in two trips collected over 200 new species of plants and trees. They included the sitka spruce, now by far the commonest tree in new plantations. He also introduced the Douglas fir, which was named after him. The Royal Scottish Forestry Society was formed in 1854, and in 1885 another Duke of Atholl planted the first Japanese larch, now an important species in Scotland.

With the spread of the British Empire and an apparent super-abundance of timber, commercial planting at home slowed down. A number of far-sighted individuals became concerned at this, and a Royal Commission recommended in 1909 that a national plan for afforestation should seek to cover nine million acres of Britain with trees within the next sixty years. In Scotland, men such as Lord Lovat and Sir John Stirling-Maxwell carried out experiments in planting conifers on poor wet ground and at relatively high altitudes, using different planting methods and pioneering the use of fertilisers.

It was, however, too little and too late. The First World War made massive demands on the nation's timber resources. Little was spared, and at the end of the war most of the trees planted between 1750 and 1850 were gone. Recognising that this was inevitable, a government committee headed by Sir Francis Acland had already met to decide what should be done. The result was a national forest policy, to be carried out by a new body, the Forestry Commission.

The Commission came into being in 1919 and from the start was lucky to be served by numbers of remarkable men, as it still is today. Among the first Commissioners were Sir John Stirling-Maxwell, Sir Francis Acland and Roy Robinson, a young Australian who was to serve the Commission until his death in 1952. The first chairman was Lord Lovat.

No time was lost; the need was urgent and work proceeded apace. Within two years in Scotland, 2,500 acres (1,000 ha) had been planted, a foresters' school was set up in Beauly, and the universities in Aberdeen and Edinburgh had diploma courses in forestry on their curricula. By 1927, no fewer than 55 new forests had been started or established in Scotland. At this time large areas of land were available for sale at very low prices – under £2 per acre was common. Much of the land was too poor for agriculture, but could be used for conifer planting, using the new techniques developed by the Commission's research branch.

By 1939 some 450,000 acres (182,250 ha) had been planted in Britain, but the ensuing six years of war saw further deep inroads made into the tree stock. Another Forestry Act was passed in 1945, and in Scotland in particular spectacular progress has been made in planting since then. By 1973 one million acres (405,000 ha) were under trees and with private forestry also making good progress, the percentage of land in Scotland under trees was up to 12 per cent; in Dumfries and Galloway Region it was over 20 per cent.

Methods of planting and nurturing trees are very different now from even thirty years ago. Giant crawler tractors are used to furrow the hill slopes ready for planting, and areas which would have been considered unplantable in the past can now be used – mostly for sitka spruce, a hardy conifer which grows acceptably even on poor soil. The forester's job in Scotland can be seen to be a tough one when you consider that, in the Swiss Alps, the treeline can extend up to 8,000 feet (2,450 m), whereas in Scotland planting over 1,500 feet (450 m) is uneconomic, if not downright impossible. The reason is not hard to seek; a combination of treacherous weather with strong winds, rain and bitter cold all act against sapling growth, and the acidic soils are reluctant to accept any crop.

The Forestry Commission has had its share of critics over the years, notably concerning the policy of block afforestation of closely planted conifers. Landscaping has improved greatly in recent times and is now accepted as an integral consideration in any new planting scheme. Fringe planting of different species, whether conifers such as larches or hardwoods, also softens the line.

# Recreation

The Forestry Commission has a duty to provide recreational facilities in its forests, and this it does. Walkers have generally free access, subject to the needs of forestry work, and the extensive network of forest roads, tracks and paths provides the basis for many walks, some of them waymarked. Forest offices can provide guidance and sometimes leaflets giving the routes of walks.

Other recreations taking place in forests include pony-trekking and orienteering. There are four established 'Forest Parks' in Scotland, which are described in a little more detail on page 49. A new feature of forest recreation is the provision of trails for cross-country skiing, for which forests are ideal. This can be expected to grow in the future, subject always to the unpredictability of snow cover in Scotland.

The Commission runs a number of campsites and has chalets for hire in several places. Details of these and other forest attractions can be obtained from the Information Branch, Forestry Commission, 231 Corstorphine Road, Edinburgh EH12 7AT.

# Looking Ahead

It is unlikely that tree cover in Scotland will drop below its present level in the foreseeable future. There are plans for considerably expanding the facilities for processing timber into pulp, chipboard or paper. Private owners are still enthusiastic foresters; although the Caledonian forest is reduced to a mere remnant of its historical size, sufficient regeneration and new planting is going on to ensure that future generations will have trees not merely to use as a crop, but also to admire for the magnificent natural things they are.

It is worth any visitor to Scotland making the effort to go to Rothiemurchus, Glen Affric or Rannoch to see a mature pine forest. It is a humbling experience merely to stand in such a forest and realise how long those trees have been there, living, growing and supporting a tremendous variety of wildlife, including rarer mammals such as the pine marten and wild cat. We must never again let our forests run down to the extent that we did forty years ago. Fortunately we have enlightened people working in the field of forestry to ensure that this will not happen.

# HYDROELECTRIC POWER

The development of hydroelectric power in the Scottish Highlands over the past thirty-five years has been remarkable, considering what a long history it has and how little had been done in the previous half-century.

The story is in fact nearly a hundred years old, and the first initiative came from a somewhat unexpected source. In 1890, the abbot of the Benedictine monastery in Fort Augustus installed a small water turbine at a site on the east side of Loch Ness, harnessing the rapid flow of water from the Falls of Foyers. It was the first public supply of electricity in Scotland, only eight years after Edison opened his experimental station in London – a little-known and rather extraordinary achievement.

Just six years later the site was taken over and developed by the British Aluminium Company to supply power for smelting – again, the first use of hydroelectric power in Britain for this purpose. The aluminium works closed in 1967, and in 1969 the North of Scotland Hydro Electric Board started work on an advanced scheme for a 300-megawatt station using both normal means and pumped storage to generate electricity. It now supplies about 400 million units of electricity each year to suppliers in the Inverness and Fort Augustus areas.

British Aluminium developed further hydro power schemes at Kinlochleven and Lochaber, which are still to be seen today. The first large scheme for public supply did not come until 1930, however, with the Grampian Electricity Company's Rannoch and Tummel development. The supply of electricity became a nationalised industry in 1947, bringing the North of Scotland Hydro Electric Board into being.

In the next twenty years, tremendous strides were made. By the end of 1955 there were 21 power stations in operation, and a further 20 under construction. By 1965 there were 54 main stations producing an average of 2,900 million units of electricity per year; their total capacity was over 1,000 megawatts.

The next major scheme, that at Ben Cruachan on the shores of Loch Awe, used a different system, called pumped storage. Normal hydroelectric power stations use the fall of water, often associated with dams, to generate electricity. In a pumped-storage station, energy generated at night when demand is low is used to pump water back up to a high-level reservoir so that it can be 'stored' for use at times of peak demand.

Cruachan is a 400-megawatt scheme, completed in 1966. It is a fascinating place to visit and, realising the potential interest, the Board runs bus trips along the service tunnels to the turbine room in the very heart of the mountain. Hill walkers such as myself can claim the unusual distinction of having visited Cruachan's summit and its heart! Foyers on Loch Ness, where the very first hydro power scheme was made, is now also a pumped-storage station.

## Lochs and Dams

These very large-scale works, which have led to mains electricity being made available to over 99 per cent of Scotland's population, have naturally had a dramatic effect on the landscape. Great care has always been taken in the siting of dams, power stations and other works, and the visitor today touring the areas where hydro power is generated would probably be astonished to be told that there are over 185 miles (300 km) of tunnels crossing the Highlands, linking schemes together into the four main areas designated by the Board.

New lochs have been created, for example, Loch Faskally near Pitlochry, crossed by the A9, and Loch Errochty above Rannoch. Dams have appeared not only on lochs, but also high on mountains such as Ben Cruachan. Power stations have been constructed in remote areas – whenever possible of local stone, at least on the facing, and sited so as to intrude as little as possible on the landscape. There have none the less been some battles with conservationists, and a scheme planned for Glen Nevis was abandoned as being environmentally undesirable after protests. All the electricity generated naturally has to be carried to the consumers, and overhead power lines have made their own statement as they march across hill and glen. They reach over 2,000 feet (600 m) at the Lecht summit near Tomintoul and on the Corrieyairack Pass between Fort Augustus and Speyside. I would not agree with one commentator who said these pylons have 'their own skeletal beauty', but we do need our power. In the most highly sensitive areas, it has sometimes been possible to lay the cables under the ground, although this is an expensive operation.

The North of Scotland Hydro Electric Board has done a remarkable job in taking power from an element present in abundance in Scotland – water – and making it available to virtually the entire population, however remote their dwelling or business. Fuller details of the network are given in the Board's own booklet *Power from the Glens*.

Another type of facility is provided, not for people, but for fish. One of the requirements of the Board in law is to 'have regard to the desirability of avoiding as far as possible injury to fisheries and to the stock of fish in any waters'. The Board has gone beyond this remit in developing fish passes and fish locks that enable salmon and sea trout to return to their spawning grounds, and in making waters available for anglers. The fish pass at Pitlochry has become a noted tourist attraction, but it is only one of many. It is 1,000 feet (310 m) long and has 34 pools, including three large 'resting' pools. There are three openings through the dam at the top of the pass, at different levels, so there is always a way out for the fish into Loch Faskally.

# WILDLIFE

## Mammals

Like other aspects of the countryside, Scotland's wildlife has changed over the centuries. A thousand years ago our indigenous species included the elk, beaver, wild boar and wolf. The last-named did not finally disappear until the middle of the eighteenth century. In the two centuries that followed there was hunting, trapping and killing on a very large scale, including everything from otters to red deer. Despite this, Scotland's mammals in particular have shown remarkable resilience and today's range of species compares with that of any other European country.

Largest of our mammals is the deer, which occurs in five varieties. The red deer, originally a forest animal, has had to adapt to life on the heather moorlands, staying at high altitude in the summer months and coming much lower down to find food in the winter. There are probably around 250,000 red deer in Scotland, of which about 40,000 are culled as part of estate management each year. Stags are stalked from August to mid-October and hinds from the end of the stag season to mid-February.

It is a thrilling experience to visit a glen with a large deer population in September or October, not just because the beasts themselves make a fine sight, but because this is the time of the rut, when the stags throw out their deep-voiced challenge as they try to gather some hinds around them for mating. Large stags may fight, clashing antlers with a loud smack. This is the only time of year when the sexes mingle. After mating they separate again, and the calves are born in May or June.

Roe deer, smaller than the red deer, are widely distributed on the mainland and on some islands, including Skye and Islay. They prefer to inhabit woodland and have caused considerable problems to foresters, as the amount of planting has increased in recent years. The Forestry Commission now has a roe deer management policy so that the deer can survive without being unduly persecuted for doing what comes naturally to them. Roes mate in August, but because of delayed implantation the fawns are not born until the following spring. They are reddish in colour in the summer and turn to a grey-brown in winter.

Fallow deer were once widely kept in estate 'parks' but now they run wild as well. They can be seen in the Borders, Perthshire, Argyll and Wester Ross. They, like roe deer, prefer woodland cover, though they will lie up in bracken if no tree cover is available. The distinctive fawny shading with prominent spots enables them to be picked out from other deer types; it also gives them excellent natural camouflage.

There are two more exotic types of deer in Scotland. The small sika, introduced from Japan, have, like fallow deer, spread from parks to become established in the wild in several areas. Sika are often a similar colour to red deer, though rather smaller, but they can be identified by the reddish velvet on their antlers, tipped with black. During the rut (September to November) the stags issue a distinctive whistle.

Reindeer, once an indigenous species, were reintroduced to the Cairngorms in the 1950s, and the herd thrives today thanks to careful management. Visitors can see them being fed at certain times of the year. They have a very distinctive head, quite unlike other deer types.

The Scottish wild cat population decreased during the nineteenth and early twentieth century, but has since grown again and these distinctive and beautiful animals can now be found over a wide area from Perth and Argyll northwards. You will be lucky, however, to spot a cat in the wild, as they are shy of man and inhabit forests and rocky hill areas where they are hard to track down. Wild cats eat mostly small mammals such as mice and voles, but will also take rabbits. Their kittens sometimes fall prey to eagles and foxes.

The fox, adaptable and resourceful, has withstood all efforts to hunt it out of existence. Deeply disliked by sheep farmers, the fox undoubtedly does considerable damage to the young lamb population each spring, but it will find food wherever it can, even moving into urban areas if necessary. Foxes are hunted by terriers in some parts of Scotland and also snared, shot, trapped and poisoned. Despite this, they survive in large numbers. Foxes often spend considerable periods of time in trees, lying unseen 15-20 feet (5-6 m) above the ground.

Other land mammals include the elusive and beautiful pine marten, which again has recovered from a position of near extinction, as its natural habitat in the pine forest was decimated. Its relatives are the weasel, stoat and polecat – the last is officially extinct in Scotland, but has been seen in so many places that it must be included – badgers, both red and grey squirrels, mountain hares – a lovely sight in their white winter coats – and the mink, an escapee from captivity, which is a considerable nuisance in some places as it kills domestic hens apparently just for the fun of it.

There are wild goats in many places in Scotland, although they too tend to shun man and are not always easy to find. Loch Lomondside has a herd, and they are stalked in some places.

Two water-loving mammals that visitors love to see are the otter and the seal. Seals are a very common sight off the Scottish coasts and round the islands. They are naturally inquisitive and their shiny black or grey heads can be seen popping up out of the water to see what's going on. Common seals can also be seen lying on rocky islets or on sand or shingle banks. Scotland is home to a large proportion of the world's grey seal population, the largest breeding colonies being in the northern islands of North Rona and the Orkneys.

The otter is well established in Scotland, though there is still cause for concern as to the overall size of the population. Things are better here, none the less, than in England and Wales, where it is estimated there may be as few as 300 otters in the wild in all. Otters are mainly found on the western seaboard and around the islands. They travel considerable distances, both in the water and over land, and will switch from one waterway to another for reasons that we do not fully understand. The belief that they are a menace to game fish is not really supported by fact; otters eat a wide range of food from eels to frogs and also small mammals such as voles.

To be lucky enough to come across an otter, or even better a family, and see them playing in the water is a wonderful experience. They genuinely enjoy play, rolling over and over and juggling with small pebbles, crabs and the like. There has been a much greater awareness of the need to conserve the otter population in recent years, fed partly by the remarkable books of Gavin Maxwell (*Ring of Bright Water* being probably the best known). The Otter Trust, based in Suffolk, does splendid work for this lovely creature.

## Birds

The bird that every visitor to the Scottish Highlands wants to see is the golden eagle. The population is currently quite healthy at around 400 birds, but they still occupy a vast area of country and for the visitor a sighting is still a rare and thrilling event. After dozens of visits to the Highlands, I still count less than ten definite sightings.

Many 'eagles' seen at a distance are in fact buzzards. The buzzard is another fine bird of prey, and much commoner than the eagle in Scotland. Its unmistakable 'mew' gives it away; and if you see two or more birds together, they are much more likely to be buzzards than eagles. My finest eagle sightings have all come high in the mountains, when I was probably near to an eyrie without realising it, whereas I have frequently seen buzzards in glens.

Even rarer is the magnificent sea eagle, reintroduced from Norway to the island of Rum in the past decade in an experiment conducted with great care and skill by staff of the Nature Conservancy Council. A small number of birds have been released from Rum and within the next few years it is hoped that they will establish themselves on other islands and on the western seaboard. Sea eagles are just as superb in flight as their land-based cousins, but are quite unmistakable with their square-cut wings and white tail feathers. They were not inaptly, but somewhat ungracefully, described to me by an NCC warden as 'like a flying plank'.

Another remarkable bird of the high mountains is the ptarmigan. Camouflaged white in winter and hard to see even in summer against a rocky background, their coughing call can come as quite a shock, as they rarely bother to move until you are a few metres away. Ptarmigan are among the birds which will put on a broken-wing act to lead you away from a nest or chicks. They are very hardy, staying at high level in the harshest winter weather.

Other birds of the hills include the glossy raven, often seen circling above crags and heard croaking from some way off, the superb peregrine falcon, a comparative rarity whose 'stoop' on to prey is one of the most thrilling sights of the avian world, and the osprey, another bird whose conservation has been very carefully monitored. The 'hides' for viewing osprey at Loch Garten in the Spey Valley and Loch of the Lowes near Dunkeld are world-famous and well worth a visit if you are in the area.

Smaller birds familiar to the hill walker include the wheatear, with its white rump, the pipit, the ring ouzel (the mountain blackbird), and the stonechat. And of course the grouse, both black and red. Few days in the hills pass without the walker being told crossly to 'go back, go back' by this bird of the heather moors. Grouse are shot in the late summer and early autumn, the 'glorious 12th' of August heralding the start of the season and a rush to get grouse on the menu at hotels from Edinburgh to London. Grouse are much less common in the western Highlands than they are in the east, where their staple diet of young heather cloaks the hills more thickly. The much larger capercaillie is mostly a denizen of forests, and makes an impressive sight.

Scotland's seabird population is varied and splendid. The cliffs of the east coast, including such wonderful places as the Bullers of Buchan, will give sightings of many thousands of birds including gannets, gulls of many types, guillemots, fulmars and kittiwakes. The northern isles are also renowned for their birdlife, with reserves at Fair Isle, Handa and other places. All around the coast the plaintive call of the oystercatcher will be heard and its bright orange beak seen. The slow, measured flight of the heron is another common sight for the observant visitor.

This is the merest outline of Scotland's rich birdlife; space will not permit a fuller listing, but there are many excellent books available to help the bird-watcher, and the bird organisations such as the RSPB also have helpful literature.

I have covered mammals and birds here, as they are the species the majority of visitors will most easily see. Wildlife extends of course far beyond them, to fish, insects, flowers and all the incredible variety of forms that nature makes to inhabit the earth. For the enquiring visitor, I highly recommend a splendid book called simply *Wildlife of Scotland*, edited by Professor Fred Holliday and published by Macmillan in paperback. It is superbly written and illustrated, and will provide you with many hours of pleasure as well as increasing your knowledge and understanding of the terrain and wildlife of Scotland.

C

*Ben Nevis and Fort William, Highland*

# CONSERVATION

## A Brief History

There is general agreement that man's finest works of art, whether temporal or spiritual in inspiration, should be conserved. Indeed, the suggestion that they should not seems slightly shocking and would be labelled as 'barbarous' and 'uncivilised' if it were made now. Thus we go to considerable lengths to keep our treasures of painting, sculpture, literature, music and architecture safe so that they can be enjoyed by our own and by future generations. When such treasures change hands, they fetch enormous sums of money. We are quite happy, too, for the state to contribute through the Arts Council, grants for museums or historic buildings, and so on.

The movement to conserve the best of our countryside is much more recent, and I think it is fair to say that it meets with more opposition than art conservation ever has. Although considerable efforts had been made to 'improve' the natural appearance of the land by way of tree planting and the laying out of 'parks' on great estates in the seventeenth and eighteenth centuries, the appreciation of landscape – especially the mountainous areas – for its own sake did not really get under way until the mid-nineteenth century.

Poets and historical novelists, including Wordsworth, Coleridge, Keats and Sir Walter Scott, were early in drawing public attention to the delights of Scotland's countryside. Queen Victoria was a great lover of the hills and glens and made some surprisingly arduous treks across them, usually on ponies, but sometimes walking too. In the latter part of the nineteenth century the railways started pushing up into the Highlands; roads were improved, and the number of tourists increased steadily.

At the same time an emigré Scot, John Muir, was discovering the great wilderness areas of the western United States, and played a considerable part in the establishment of the National Park movement there. The world's first National Park, Yellowstone Park, was opened in 1872. There seemed to be little cause for concern this side of the Atlantic. Scotland was a very large, wild area of country, and surely the hand of man could not make sufficient impact on the land to spoil it? Much of the land was in the hands of the great estate owners, either titled men and women or the *nouveaux riches* such as the Bullough family, who sealed off the island of Rum as their private reserve and built the fantasy Kinloch Castle of pink Arran sandstone, complete with extravagant Oriental fitments, central heating, electric light and a heated turtle pond – and this was in 1902!

Such 'battles' as there were centred on rights of way, and tribute must be paid to the Scottish Rights of Way Society for its great work in keeping through-routes open when landowners tried to close them off. An offshoot of this was Scottish MP James Bryce's Access to Mountains Bill, proposed in 1884, over a hundred years ago. It was vigorously opposed by landowning interests in Parliament and did not succeed.

In the sixty years that followed Bryce's attempted Bill, numerous further attempts were made to 'formalise' countryside legislation. There were calls for National Parks in Britain throughout the 1920s and 1930s, supported by the impetus of the newly-formed rambling and youth hostelling bodies, but it was after the Second World War that hope was translated into action.

In 1945, two committees reported to Parliament. The report prepared by John Dower led eventually to the setting up of the ten National Parks currently established in England and Wales. In Scotland, the committee chaired by Sir Douglas Ramsay recommended the creation of five National Parks, totalling nearly 1,870 square miles (500,000 ha) of superb landscape. The areas were Loch Lomond and the Trossachs; Glen Affric/Glen Cannich/ Strathfarrar; Ben Nevis, Glencoe and the Blackmount; the Cairngorms; Torridon/Loch Maree/Little Loch Broom.

The popular feeling that ran so strongly in England and Wales to establish National Parks did not rise in Scotland, and all that happened was that these five areas were designated as National Park Direction Areas, giving them a sketchy protection in that major developments were subject to scrutiny by the government. This does not mean that nothing was being done on the ground. The National Trust for Scotland had already acquired several large areas, including Glencoe, and by declaring them inalienable, it was able to control development very effectively. The first Forest Park, Argyll, was set up in 1935; and the Nature Conservancy was establishing reserves in a number of places.

The National Trust for Scotland took another initiative in 1961, when it commissioned the eminent mountaineer and writer W. H. Murray to survey Highland landscapes and report on those which were felt to be the most worthy of conservation. He not only did this, nominating 21 areas, but also described in pungent terms the threats to the landscape which had occurred and were still occurring. One of these threats – a plan for damming Glen Nevis – had led to the commissioning of the report, but the project was fortunately later dropped.

Murray did not mince his words. This, of the Hydro Electric Board, is typical:

It is inevitable that the works of human organisation, possessed of too much power, should be unequal. Thus the magnificent work done by the Board in Glen Affric, when in defiance of all prognostication they left the land clean of scars, save for one dam, and that not too unsightly, is offset by the cut-price job in Glen Cannich, of which nothing good can be said. So it is throughout the country, the good and bad alternate.

(Remember that Glen Cannich was at that time in a National Park Direction Area.) Murray ended the introduction to his report in these memorable words:

> The outstanding beauty of the Highland scene, which is one of the nation's great natural assets, has been haphazardly expended and no account kept. The wasting away of this asset is bound to continue and to accelerate unless discrimination and control are brought to bear by some body created for the purpose and granted powers by government, so that checks and safeguards may be instituted. If action to that good end be not taken now, the Scottish people will lose by neglect what remains of their natural heritage.

W. H. Murray's report, called simply *Highland Landscape*, was published by the National Trust for Scotland in 1962. In his foreword, the Trust's then Chairman, the Earl of Wemyss and March (now its President), expressed the hope that the 21 areas would become as well known, as 'Murrays', as the individual mountains were known as 'Munros'.

This has not happened, but within five years of the report appearing, and with many other people expressing concern over the conservation of the countryside, there was action. The Countryside (Scotland) Act of 1967 established the Countryside Commission for Scotland as an agency of central government. Its aims and role are more fully discussed below, on page 41.

The Commission is constantly consulted on matters relating to conservation, but two of its many reports have had particularly far-reaching effects. *A Park System for Scotland* (1974) suggested a four-tier structure which would comprise a basic component of a comprehensive recreational strategy. Three of the tiers – urban parks, country parks and regional parks – are now recognised by statute. The fourth tier, that of special parks, has not been proceeded with to date. The Commission also recognised that, in its own words, 'there are areas in Scotland of outstanding scenic importance in national and even international terms which are not under great recreational pressure at present and which it might therefore not be appropriate to designate as parks within a recreational system'. This is a rare recognition of the fact that designation can of itself help to destroy that which it serves to protect, by attracting people. Call an area a 'wilderness' and people will want to go and see what it looks like.

The Commission's second major report, *Scotland's Scenic Heritage*, appeared in 1978. It followed a study more exhaustive than W. H. Murray's and identified no less than 40 areas worthy of conservation and protection. These areas, which are listed on pages 49-54, are now designated as National Scenic Areas. They range from coastal Dumfriesshire to the Orkney and Shetland Islands, and even out to St Kilda, and in character from the machair of Uist to the wild ruggedness of north-west Sutherland or the Cairngorms. In these areas, planning authorities must consult the Commission in all cases where proposed development within six specific classes is likely to have a significant effect on scenic interest. These six specific areas of concern are:

1. schemes for five or more houses, flats or chalets except for those within towns and villages for which specific proposals have been made in an adopted local plan;
2. sites for five or more mobile dwellings or caravans;
3. all non-residential developments requiring more than 1.2 acres (0.5 ha) of land, excluding agricultural and forestry developments;
4. all buildings and structures over 40 feet (12 m) high, including agricultural and forestry developments;
5. vehicle tracks over 1,000 feet (300 m) in altitude, except where these form part of an afforestation proposal which has been agreed by the planning authority;
6. all local highway authority roadworks outside present road boundaries costing more than £100,000.

There were those who felt that agricultural and forestry bodies should not have been largely excluded from these provisions, and there is certainly ground for concern in this area.

A further Act of Parliament – the Countryside (Scotland) Act of 1981 – enabled planning authorities or the Commission to make management agreements with private landowners. These agreements can help to conserve land in the interests of scenic conservation and ensure public access, in return for which the landowner receives a compensatory payment.

That, briefly, is the formal position at present, although as with all legislation there is much more to it than I can set down here. What of the voluntary sector? Here, too, great strides have been made, which can be summarised under three headings – advice, information/education and action.

## Advice

There are now many voluntary organisations operating in the general area of 'countryside conservation'. They have within their ranks considerable expertise, and their help and advice is often sought on matters relating to the landscape, its flora and fauna. A fuller list of these bodies can be found in the section headed 'Who Does What' on page 170.

Bodies such as the Scottish Wildlife Trust and the Royal Society for the Protection of Birds work closely with the national agencies, and have played a considerable role in setting up and maintaining nature reserves, in researching the extent and habitats of wild creatures, and in helping to draft protective legislation.

Bodies with a wider brief, such as the Association for the Protection of Rural Scotland and the Scottish Countryside Activities Council, also have a most useful role to play in acting as forums, bringing together people of different interests and disciplines, but with common ground in their love of and concern for the countryside. The Saltire Society also comes into this category.

Mountaineering and walking have their own representative bodies, as do other forms of recreation from orienteering to game fishing. And let us not forget the pressure groups. They may often be seen as an irritant in officialdom's side, but their concern and their views are genuine and they would not exist if they felt there was no need for their separate voice to be heard.

# Information/Education

Many of the bodies referred to above issue publications which aim to inform or to educate in matters relating to some aspect of the countryside. Some hold meetings, conferences or run courses where the general public can learn more about wildlife, ecology, geology or related subjects. The Countryside Commission for Scotland's helpful free booklet *Who's Who* gives more information on which bodies do what in this area.

Environmental education in a more formal sense is perhaps less widely available. The Scottish Field Studies Association runs excellent courses at its field centre near Blairgowrie, and many education authorities organise field trips for secondary school-children. The countryside ranger service, developed under the aegis of the Commission, has an important role to play here too. As in so many other areas of life, teaching children to respect and enjoy the countryside cannot start too early, although the teaching needs to be gentle and not forcibly applied!

Some of the voluntary bodies, such as RSPB, have junior sections which do an excellent job in awakening and maintaining interest in things natural. The work of the Aigas Field Centre, near Beauly, is worthy of mention; they have taken children from deprived inner-city areas and opened their eyes to wonders they never knew existed.

There is always more to be done in the fields of information and education, but luckily there is no shortage of willing folk eager to transmit to others the knowledge they have acquired and the pleasure they get from the natural world.

# Action

Anyone with an urge to translate a desire to conserve into practical work can be accommodated too. Perhaps notably in this field, the Scottish Conservation Projects Trust operates week-long 'tasks' throughout Scotland between spring and autumn, tackling anything from scrub clearance to draining silted-up ponds and making or stabilising paths. Their address is given on page 173 and they are always looking for more willing hands.

The National Trust for Scotland's junior wing, Youth in Trust, runs similar task forces, as do a number of the conservation and wildlife bodies. Schools, too, encourage their pupils to take an interest in practical countryside work through tree planting or 'adopting' a local area and keeping it tidy.

# Is It All Enough?

It might seem from the above that a great deal is being done in the field of countryside conservation in Scotland. So it is, but I am still uneasy about the overall situation. The government agencies do not, I feel, have strong enough powers to stop large developments. There is a very great need for a 'holding' body that could acquire land of national scenic interest or importance – say, a large part of one of the 40 NSAs – if it came on to the market. If this were possible, the seller would receive his money and the area's future could be discussed without undue pressure of time.

There is also, to my mind, a need for less secrecy over countryside developments. More openness and more debate at an early stage would harm no one and could be of great benefit. One of the reasons why some conservation bodies in Scotland have been accused of 'always opposing development' is that they consistently hear about these developments too late to offer sensible alternative proposals, and then feel that opposition is the only course left. The result, as with the Cairngorms ski development, is a long and very expensive public inquiry and unnecessary acrimony on both sides. There need, in fact, be no 'sides'. There is room, surely, for all points of view to be put and heard, and for wise judgements to be made, taking a long view of things.

*Scotland's Scenic Heritage* summarises the matter well. The Countryside Commission for Scotland says in its introduction:

> The countryside should be seen as a place of great beauty and attractiveness in its own right to be enjoyed by the people who live and work in Scotland. It is the nation's responsibility to watch over and cherish this asset and to pass it on to future generations in a way which will show that proper care and concern have been taken to accommodate new developments and to retain the natural attractiveness and amenity which the community has inherited from its predecessors.

That responsibility lies with each one of us; it is a challenge to which we should not be slow to rise.

# The Countryside Commission for Scotland

The Countryside Commission for Scotland was established in 1968, under the powers made available to the Secretary of State by the passing of the Countryside (Scotland) Act a year earlier. It is an advisory and promotional body, funded from government sources, and has five main aims. These are:

to conserve and enhance the natural beauty of Scotland's countryside;
to help provide, develop and improve facilities for the enjoyment of the countryside;
to increase public understanding and awareness and to promote proper use of the countryside;
to provide a factual base for determining policy and for carrying out practical work in the field;
to update policies and practices and to keep abreast of current developments.

How are these aims achieved? The Commission's staff have skills and qualifications covering many disciplines – architecture, planning, landscape design, land use, teaching, graphic design, and other related subjects. They report to the Countryside Commissioners, a body of 12 men and women who are appointed by the Secretary of State and who give their service, sometimes extending over many years, on a voluntary basis. They are led by a Chairman who receives a small salary.

The Commission can on occasion take a leading role in some special activity by setting up development projects to demonstrate to others what can be done. The training of rangers is also undertaken by the Commission. In general, however, it aims to give assistance and funds to enable others to carry out their own programmes of work connected with the countryside. To this end it co-operates with both statutory bodies (for example, local authorities, the Forestry Commission, the Highlands and Islands Development Board) and voluntary organisations (such as the Scottish Wildlife Trust, the National Trust for Scotland, the Scottish Conservation Projects Trust), giving them advice where requested and grants where it is deemed appropriate.

The work of the Countryside Commission is considered below, under the five headings related to the aims listed earlier.

*Protection*

The Commission has to advise the Secretary of State and planning authorities on planning matters within the countryside (over 98 per cent of

*The Cairngorms, Grampian*

the land and inland water of Scotland is designated as countryside). Among the cases on which the Commission has been consulted are large-scale industrial developments, on-shore oil-related sites, coastal power stations, new roads, reservoirs, mineral workings and overhead power lines.

Consideration is given to the physical, social and economic character of localities, landscape design and the possible after-effects of the proposals. Even with small-scale developments, attention to design and detail can make all the difference between a development which fits comfortably into its surroundings and one which does not.

The Commission seeks to influence policies at central and local government levels. It also prepares advice notes on countryside planning and management to help local authorities and other bodies.

## Recreational Provision

This work is done mainly by local authorities, who can obtain grants of up to 75 per cent from the Commission for the provision of recreational facilities (100 per cent for work on designated long-distance footpaths). Grants are made to voluntary bodies and private landowners for similar work. Grants can be made for a very wide range of things – car parks, toilets, improvements to youth hostels, provision of country parks and regional parks, picnic sites, reception and interpretation centres, improvement to footpaths, tree planting, and so on. Annual grants are made each year towards the countryside ranger service, which is considered in more detail below (see page 45).

The Commission's role in all this work is to help provide a range of well-sited facilities designed and constructed to a high standard and to ensure that problems such as fire risk or erosion are considered at the planning stage.

## Conservation Education

The aim here is to help people of all ages to enjoy the countryside safely and at the same time to develop a positive interest in its conservation. This can be done by providing interpretive facilities at visitor centres, at scenic viewpoints, and on guided walks and trails. It can also be achieved by giving advice to teachers and encouraging properly prepared fieldwork for students.

The Commission's main contribution is to help and advise people planning these provisions and to provide training for those who design and operate facilities for visitors at countryside properties. Training courses were started in 1969 and have developed considerably since then. Staff come to the Commission's training centre at Battleby, near Perth, from national agencies, local authorities, voluntary organisations and private landowners to attend the courses which the Commission runs for countryside rangers. A wide range of publications is available, including material for schools and youth organisations.

*Research and Development*

The aim of the Commission's research work is to provide a factual basis for practical advice to local authorities and others. This can be done by exploring the nature of planning problems, seeking new solutions and devising plans for recreational provision relating to the long-term conservation of our national scenic heritage. Surveys on particular topics such as the design of buildings or the construction of footbridges are also undertaken. Early in 1985, detailed analyses of a major survey into leisure in the countryside were published, showing that millions of trips into the Scottish countryside were made every year, indicating people's preferences and providing the Commission with valuable information for its future work.

Development work has ranged from schemes for managing loch shores and coastal beaches and demonstrating the value of ranger services in the Highlands to environmental improvement and promoting the use of canals for recreation in the Central Belt. At Battleby, a countryside display shows items such as picnic benches, litter bins, stiles, signs and waymarks, and methods of car park and pathway construction.

*Review*

The fifth of the Commission's main aims is that of keeping all policy matters affecting the countryside under review – for example, in regard to the identification of areas which might require special protection or could be used for recreational development.

The Commission has published proposals for a recreational park system for Scotland (*A Park System for Scotland*), parts of which are now being implemented. Another survey report has identified 40 areas which should be safeguarded, and which are now designated as National Scenic Areas, with provision for the Commission to be consulted before any major development takes place.

*Summary*

In presenting one of its recent Annual Reports, its Chairman, Mr David Nickson, CBE, said: 'The Commission has a very difficult – and very worthwhile – job to do in advising government on planning issues and in promoting sound policies for the balanced productive use, enjoyment and conservation of our countryside. We have nothing to hide and much, I believe, of which to be proud.'

That report showed that in the year under review no less than £2.6 million had been given in countryside grants to local authorities, voluntary bodies and the private sector. The Countryside Commission for Scotland will continue to pursue its aims firmly, to ensure that its funds are wisely spent, and to encourage the provision of facilities which increase our ability to enjoy and understand the countryside where we take our leisure.

## Countryside Rangers

As you travel about the Scottish countryside, you will almost certainly sooner or later encounter a countryside ranger. There are many misconceptions about the role of rangers and what powers they have, and I hope this short section will leave you with a better understanding of their work and how they can be of help to the visitor.

As you have read in the previous section, the ranger service in Scotland has been developed with very great encouragement and guidance from the Countryside Commission for Scotland, and courses for rangers are held regularly at the Commission's headquarters at Battleby, near Perth. If rangers are employed under the terms laid down by the Countryside (Scotland) Act, the Commission pays a proportion of their salary as grant-aid, whether they are employed by local authorities, voluntary bodies or on private estates.

What is the ranger's job? First, to provide information, help and advice to visitors and to show us how we can enjoy the countryside with as little disturbance as possible to wildlife and to other land uses such as farming or forestry. Rangers can also provide assistance in emergencies – some are members of mountain rescue teams, for instance – and have a very important role to play in supervising and helping to carry out conservation work in the countryside.

The ranger is the 'man (or woman) in the middle', between the landowner or land-user and the visitor. He works very much as a liaison officer, assisting in initial negotiation for such things as footpath agreements, where the local authority may be asking the landowner to co-operate over the route of a long-distance or recreational path. The ranger, being out and about all the time, will almost certainly know the landowner or farmer concerned and can make the initial approach on a personal basis.

Many rangers have particular practical skills, such as drystone dyking, or have developed a knowledge of wildlife or flora which they put to very good use when leading guided walks. Such walks are advertised locally and it is always worth enquiring at tourist information centres for details. They can be particularly good for children in helping them to explore the natural world and in giving them a first understanding of the need for conservation of our landscape and wild places. Many rangers give talks in the winter to schools and to bodies such as the SWRI. Increasingly, too, they are providing for disabled visitors in the countryside.

Remember, if you come across a ranger, that he or she is there to help you. Do not be afraid to ask advice. A note here may avoid some confusion for visitors. Some bodies, such as the Nature Conservancy Council, use the word warden instead of ranger. Basically the job is very similar. Rangers in Scotland have their own organisation (Scottish Countryside Rangers Association) and hold a study conference each year, as well as sending delegates to the conference run by the Association of Countryside Rangers in England.

# THE PARK SYSTEM

In December 1974, the Countryside Commission for Scotland published a discussion document entitled *A Park System for Scotland*. The document proposed four 'levels' of designated or recognised parks as being appropriate within Scotland. Of these, three – urban or local parks, country parks, and regional parks – have been established by statute, but the question of the fourth category, that of 'special park', has not been resolved.

It will be noted that the term 'national park', as applied to ten areas in England and Wales, does not appear. This is deliberate; in the discussion document's words, 'the Commission does not suggest the setting up in Scotland of National Parks in the internationally accepted sense'. It was felt that the local authorities – regional and district councils – should maintain their major role as determiners of development policy and planning control, and not forfeit that role to a new national agency.

A separate category, that of 'forest park', has been in existence since 1935. Forest parks are areas owned by the Forestry Commission where considerable provision is made for recreation. There are four in Scotland, and they are listed below (see also the section on Forestry above).

## Local or Urban Parks

These, as their name implies, are usually in urban or at least populated areas. Generally, they do not provide specific 'countryside' recreation and are therefore not included in this book. Some country parks were formerly 'urban' parks, such as Pollok Park in Glasgow.

## Country Parks

The Countryside (Scotland) Act of 1967 defines a country park as 'a park or pleasure ground in the countryside which by reason of its position in relation to major concentrations of population affords convenient opportunities to the public for enjoyment of the countryside or open-air recreation'. There are, at the time of writing, 32 country parks in Scotland, in very varied locations, from coastal sites to urban fringe. They offer the opportunity for many different kinds of recreation, or you can simply enjoy a walk, or watch the wildlife. The parks are listed in the Gazetteer.

# Regional Parks

Statutory provision for the designation of regional parks was provided in the Countryside (Scotland) Act of 1981. They are intended to provide a comprehensive system of public access to the countryside, ranging from areas of low use to heavily used sites. They may include one or more country parks within their boundaries, linked by footpaths or other areas over which access agreements have been negotiated. They will normally cover fairly large areas, including areas where agriculture or forestry are the principal land uses.

The first of these parks was the Clyde/Muirshiel Regional Park, set up by Renfrew County Council and now operated by Strathclyde Region – though not yet formally designated. It includes the country parks at Castle Semple and Muirshiel.

# Special Parks

There are at present no designated 'special parks' in Scotland. It is possible that in the foreseeable future the area covered by the Loch Lomond Plan may receive such designation. In the 1974 study, the Commission proposed three areas as being suitable for such designation – the Cairngorms, Glen Nevis/Glencoe, and Loch Lomond/Trossachs.

It is interesting at this point to look back at the recommendations of the Ramsay Report in 1945. It proposed the setting up of five national parks in Scotland, as follows:

Ben Nevis/Glencoe/Blackmount (610 sq miles/158,000 ha)
Cairngorms (180 sq miles/46,600 ha)
Glen Affric/Glen Cannich/Strathfarrar (260 sq miles/67,350 ha)
Loch Lomond/Trossachs (320 sq miles/82,900 ha)
Loch Torridon/Loch Maree/Little Loch Broom (500 sq miles/129,500 ha)

You will note that three of these areas have, in broad terms, been seen as suitable for 'special park' designation. Three 'reserve' national park areas were also designated. These were Moidart/Morar/Knoydart; Glen Lyon/Ben Lawers/Schiehallion; and St Mary's Loch, in the Borders.

Legislation to establish these national parks was never enacted, but the five main areas were subject to National Park Direction Orders, which required the local authorities to submit all planning applications for development within these areas to the Secretary of State for Scotland. In 1980, these NPDOs were repealed and the areas incorporated into the system of National Scenic Areas.

# Forest Parks

Forest Parks have been set up by the Forestry Commission in four large areas. They embrace not only forested land, but also mountains, moorland and extensive tracts of water. Recreational provision is available for walking, climbing, sailing, canoeing, orienteering, horse-riding, camping and other activities, and the Commission also has chalets available for hire.

*Argyll Forest Park*

This, the first of the breed, was established as long ago as 1935. It covers 100 square miles (25,900 ha) in the Arrochar and Cowal area, including the sea lochs that run up from the north side of the Clyde estuary.

*Galloway Forest Park*

Set up in 1945, this park extends for 200 square miles (51,800 ha) and includes the forests of Carrick, Clatteringshaws, Glen Trool, Garraries and Kirroughtree. Within the park is the Merrick, at 2,764 feet (830 m) the highest hill in southern Scotland.

*Glen More Forest Park*

Centred on the Queen's Forest above the Spey Valley and close to the Cairngorm ski grounds, the park was opened in 1947, and is the smallest of the four at just 20 square miles (5,180 ha). It includes Loch Morlich, and an unusual feature in the forest is a network of cross-country ski trails.

*Queen Elizabeth Forest Park*

The most recent to be established, it commemorates the 1953 coronation and extends to 60 square miles (15,550 ha) in the Trossachs area. It covers Ben Lomond and the Trossachs forests of Achray and includes the information centre at David Marshall Lodge near Aberfoyle.

For futher information, write to the Forestry Commission, 231 Corstorphine Road, Edinburgh EH12 7AT.

# National Scenic Areas (NSAs)

Following the publication of *A Park System for Scotland*, the Countryside Commission for Scotland set in hand a review of the Scottish landscape to identify areas worthy of conservation as being part of the national heritage.

The subsequent report, *Scotland's Scenic Heritage*, was published in 1978 and identified 40 areas as being of outstanding merit on the grounds of scenic beauty and attractiveness.

It is interesting to note that in the survey he carried out in 1961 on behalf of the National Trust for Scotland (the Countryside Commission for Scotland was not in being then, of course), the eminent mountaineer and writer W. H. Murray visited 52 areas and selected 21 as being of outstanding quality. His selection overlaps to a great degree with the 40 national scenic areas, but whereas he was concerned exclusively with high land, the Commission's study went further, taking in coastal areas and parts of the Borders and lowland Scotland.

The designated areas are listed below. You will not find anything 'different' about them if you visit them – no signs indicating their designation, or facilities related to that fact, but I am sure you will agree that they are fully worthy of conservation in the best sense.

*Borders*

*Eildon and Leaderfoot* (8,900 acres/3,600 ha): the area around Melrose including the Eildon Hills and Black Hill, noted for its association with Sir Walter Scott.

*Upper Tweeddale* (30,400 acres/12,300 ha): the area west of Peebles, taking in most of the Manor Valley, Drumelzier and Broughton.

*Central*

*The Trossachs* (11,350 acres/4,600 ha): centred on Loch Achray, taking in Ben Venue and Ben A'n.

Part of *Loch Lomond* NSA (see under Strathclyde).

Part of *Loch Rannoch and Glen Lyon* NSA (see under Tayside).

*Fife*

No designated areas.

*Dumfries and Galloway*

*East Stewartry Coast* (12,850 acres/5,200 ha): Mersehead Sands to Auchencairn Bay and the hinterland running up towards Dalbeattie.

*Fleet Valley* (13,100 acres/5,300 ha): Fleet Bay and the valley of the Fleet as far as the southern end of the Rig of Drumruck.

*Nith Estuary* (23,000 acres/9,300 ha): the valley and estuary of the River

Nith from just south of Dumfries to the sea, and including Criffel and Caerlaverock.

## Grampian

*The Cairngorm Mountains* (166,050 acres/67,200 ha) (part in Highland Region): the whole area from the Spey Valley (Aviemore to Loch Insh), east by Glen Feshie and the Geldie Burn, north of the Dee to Glen Avon, west to Bynack Mor and north of the Queen's Forest back to the Spey.

*Deeside and Lochnagar* (99,350 acres/40,200 ha) (part in Tayside Region): adjoining the Cairngorms area and extending east along Deeside to Ballater and south taking in the whole Lochnagar massif and the Mounth hills above Glen Doll.

## Highland

*Assynt – Coigach* (222,900 acres/90,200 ha): Eddrachillis Bay south to Little Loch Broom and inland via Cul Mor and Ben More Assynt to Loch Glendhu.

*Ben Nevis and Glencoe* (251,050 acres/101,600 ha) (part in Strathclyde): the whole Ben Nevis/Grey Corries range, the Mamores, Glencoe, Glen Etive, the Blackmount and the western part of Rannoch Moor – a vast area encompassing some of the most magnificent scenery in Scotland, and Britain's highest mountain.

*The Cuillin Hills, Skye* (54,100 acres/21,900 ha): includes the Black and Red Cuillin, Loch Scavaig and the island of Soay – a unique area beloved of mountaineers for generations.

*Dornoch Firth* (18,500 acres/7,500 ha): both sides of the firth, inland as far as Bonar Bridge.

*Glen Affric* (47,700 acres/19,300 ha): the boundary follows the ridges north of the glen from Toll Creagach to Sgurr nan Ceathreamhnan then to Beinn Fhada (Attow), Ciste Dubh, Sgurr nan Conbhairean, along and down to Loch Beinn a'Mheadhoin.

*Glen Strathfarrar* (9,400 acres/3,800 ha): the central part of the glen only, from Culligran Falls in the east to the head of Loch Beannacharan in the west, taking in the summits of Garbh-charn and Carn Ban to the north and Meall a'Mhadaidh and Carn Moraig to the south.

*Kintail* (40,300 acres/16,400 ha): adjoins Glen Affric NSA. The boundary runs from Beinn Fhada to Ciste Dubh, across Glen Shiel to Sgurr na Sgine, to the Mam Ratagan pass, around the mouth of Loch Duich and over to Glen Elchaig.

*Knoydart* (97,600 acres/39,500 ha): the whole area around Lochs Hourn and Nevis, including Beinn Sgritheall to the north, east to the Saddle and Sgurr na Sgine, south to Loch Quioch and south-west again to the watershed between Loch Nevis and Loch Morar.

*Kyle of Tongue* (45,700 acres/18,500 ha): along the coast from Torrisdale to Port Vasgo, inland around the kyle and spreading to take in Ben Hope (the most northerly Munro) and Ben Loyal.

*Loch Shiel* (33,100 acres/13,400 ha): both sides of this long and beautiful loch up to its head at Glenfinnan and as far down as Beinn Resipol, and including the fine side glen of Hurich.

*Morar, Moidart and Ardnamurchan* (39,300 acres/15,900 ha): the sound of Arisaig, the western part of Moidart and the north part of the Ardnamurchan peninsula, but not quite including the actual Point of Ardnamurchan, the most westerly point on the British mainland, or Morar itself.

*North-west Sutherland* (50,650 acres/20,500 ha): the area around Loch Laxford and inland to include the massifs of Foinaven and Arkle, after which the Duchess of Westminster named the famous racehorses.

*Trotternish* (12,350 acres/5,000 ha): Flodigarry to Grealin, including the Quiraing, Beinn Edra and Staffin Island – fantastic basalt pinnacles and spires, and 'kilt rock' sea cliffs.

*Wester Ross* (359,000 acres/145,300 ha): a huge area, taking in the coast from Gruinard Bay to Loch Gairloch and Upper Loch Torridon. Inland the boundary follows the south side of Little Loch Broom, rounds An Teallach, then runs south to Glen Docherty. It swing south-west to Achnashellach and Loch Kishorn and north across Applecross, including Beinn Bhan. All the Torridon mountains are included.

*Lothian*

No designated areas.

*Strathclyde*

*Ben Nevis and Glencoe* (see under Highland).

*Jura* (53,850 acres/21,800 ha): the whole of the island south of Loch Tarbert and the northern side of the loch up to the first summit ridges (Staon Bheinn, Cruib, Glac Mhor).

*Knapdale* (48,900 acres/19,800 ha): the Sound of Jura coast from Loch Crinan down to Loch Caolisport and inland from the head of that loch to Kilmichael Glassary.

*Kyles of Bute* (10,900 acres/4,400 ha): the lower part of Glendaruel, Loch Ruel (or Riddon) and the inner Kyles of Bute.

*Loch Lomond* (67,700 acres/27,400 ha) (part in Central Region): the whole of the loch and its surrounding hills, including Ben Lomond.

*Loch na Keal, Mull* (31,400 acres/12,700 ha): Loch na Keal and Loch Tuath, the south side of Ben More up to the summit, Ulva, Staffa, and the Treshnish Islands.

*Lynn of Lorn* (11,850 acres/4,800 ha): the island of Lismore and its islets and skerries and the mainland to the east from Shuna Island to Ardmucknish Bay.

*North Arran* (58,800 acres/23,800 ha): the whole north part of the island from Brodick Bay and Machrie Bay northwards.

*Scarba, Lunga and the Garvellachs* (4,700 acres/1,900 ha): the smallest NSA apart from St Kilda, it takes in the islands between Luing and Jura.

## Tayside

Part of *Deeside and Lochnagar* (see under Grampian).

*Loch Rannoch and Glen Lyon* (119,600 acres/48,400 ha) (small part in Central Region): Loch Rannoch, Loch Dunalastair, Schiehallion, the Black Wood of Rannoch, much of Glen Lyon, Ben Lawers and the Tarmachans.

*Loch Tummel* (22,750 acres/9,200 ha): Loch Tummel with the hills on either side, the northern part of Loch Faskally and the Linn of Tummel, and the Pass of Killiecrankie.

*River Earn* (7,400 acres/3,000 ha): the upper part of Strathearn between Comrie and St Fillans, together with the peak of Mor Bheinn.

*River Tay* (13,850 acres/5,600 ha): the area around Dunkeld – the transition from highland to lowland river, as the Tay crosses the Highland boundary fault.

## Western Isles

*St Kilda* (2,220 acres/900 ha): the smallest of the NSAs, taking in the whole group including Boreray and Levenish.

*South Lewis, Harris and North Uist* (268,350 acres/108,600 ha): the mountainous parts of south-west Lewis, all of Harris, the Sound of Harris and the northern part of North Uist.

*South Uist machair* (15,100 acres/6,100 ha): the coast from Drimsdale to the southern end of the island. The machair with its wonderful profusion of flowers is a special characteristic of the Western Isles.

*Orkney*

*Hoy and West Mainland* (36,550 acres/14,800 ha): North Hoy, Hoy Sound and part of south-west Mainland extending from Yesnaby to Ward Hill.

*Shetland*

*Shetland* (35,350 acres/14,300 ha): six separate areas, all coastal, and including Muckle Roe, Fair Isle, Foula, Esha Ness, Uyea and Herma Ness.

# RECREATION

## Walking and Climbing

I have written elsewhere that Scotland is near paradise for the hill walker, a view that strengthens as my knowledge of the country grows. If you have the time and the energy, walking is surely the best way to experience any country: the slow rhythm of your progress enables you to see all there is to see and to take in the whole scene around you, from the broad sweep of the landscape to the fine detail of its flora and fauna.

Whatever your taste in scenery, as a walker Scotland will provide it for you. For the energetic and experienced, there are nearly 300 mountains of over 3,000 feet (914 m), offering everything from broad plateaux (the Cairngorms, Angus, Glen Lyon) to sharp-toothed ridges where the hands come into play and the enjoyment of a sense of exposure is an advantage (Glencoe, Skye, Arran). There are many superb through-walks using historical routes of passage, such as the Mounth roads above Deeside, Glen Tilt and the Corrieyairack Pass, built as a military road in the eighteenth century.

Visitors less experienced in mountain walking or who wish for less of a physical challenge are equally well catered for. Forest walks abound, and short explorations of beautiful glens and lochsides can occupy your time very pleasantly. Guided walks led by countryside rangers are on offer in many areas.

The walker in Scotland is doubly fortunate; not only is the scenery among the finest in Europe, but there is, by and large, easy access to open land, with far fewer problems than are encountered in England and Wales. The hills and glens are open to visiting walkers all the year round, except for the sensible restrictions which apply on estates when shooting or stalking is in progress. The prime time for these pursuits is mid-August to mid-October, and during that time local enquiry should be made (initially at police or post offices) to ascertain if any restrictions apply. Contact with the estate stalker, where possible, is advisable.

The shooting and stalking season overlaps with that of the Highland midge. From June to September this irritating pest takes delight in torturing anybody who dares to expose bare flesh. Away from the Western Highlands it is much less virulent, and the hill walker often has the relief of climbing above its sphere of influence. It doesn't like wind and you can also escape from its attention on the coast.

There are rights of way in Scotland, but unlike England and Wales you will not find them specifically marked on Ordnance Survey maps. A right of way here is defined as a path between two places of public resort where continuous use can be proven over a period of not less than twenty years. The Scottish Rights of Way Society has been defending their existence for well over a hundred years. Although rights of way are not marked on OS maps, paths and tracks are, and a little study will reveal the unlimited possibilities for superb walking routes, particularly for the more adventurous. Rights of way remain open during the shooting and stalking season.

The extraordinary growth in 'named' long-distance walking routes that has occurred in England and Wales in recent years has not been paralleled in Scotland; with generally free access, it follows that there is less need to create such routes. The Countryside Commission for Scotland has designated three routes, and at the time of publication all three are at least partly open.

*The West Highland Way.* This runs from Milngavie, north of Glasgow, to Fort William via Strathblane, the east side of Loch Lomond, Glen Falloch, Crianlarich, Tyndrum, Bridge of Orchy, Glencoe and Kinlochleven, and is about 95 miles (150 km). HMSO guidebook: *The West Highland Way* by Robert Aitken.

*The Southern Upland Way.* This begins at Portpatrick, near Stranraer, and ends at Cockburnspath, on the Berwickshire coast, passing through the Galloway and Dumfriesshire hills, Moffat, St Mary's Loch, Traquair, Galashiels and the Lammermuir hills. It is about 210 miles (336 km). HMSO guidebook: *The Southern Upland Way* by Ken Andrew, in two volumes.

*The Speyside Way.* This footpath passes along the east side of the Spey Valley, from Spey Bay to a point near Aviemore, and is about 60 miles (100 km). Full development of this path has been held up by a dispute over the ownership of the trackbed of an old railway which it is planned to use for the southern section. The northern half is open and route leaflets are available. There is a proposal for a short coastal extension to Cullen.

In some areas, local authorities have signposted short walks, and guides to these are available at tourist information centres and local bookshops. For general guidance, the excellent series of district guides published by the Scottish Mountaineering Trust and widely available in Scotland will give more ideas than most of us could cover in a lifetime.

Equipment for walking in Scotland should be chosen with the thought in

*The Lairig Ghru, a pass in the Cairngorms running from Linn of Dee to Aviemore*

mind that conditions overhead and underfoot can *and do* change rapidly. Good waterproofs and stout footwear are essential to your comfort. It is fair to add that these very changing conditions are part of the special delight of walking in Scotland, and can provide the photographer with moments of pure magic, as light and shade shift with the cloud patterns.

The ability to read a map and use a compass will help greatly; the very best of Scotland for the walker is off the tracks in the wilder areas. You need to be competent to penetrate such areas as Knoydart and the inner Cairngorms, but the rewards are truly infinite.

*The Vertical Dimension*

Scotland is famous rock-climbing country and if you have made the step beyond scrambling to enjoying the unusual pleasures of tackling steep rock faces there is plenty to occupy you here. Climbing goes on at an intense level of activity, summer and winter. Principal climbing areas include Glencoe, the Cairngorms and Lochnagar, the vast sweep of cliff on the north side of Ben Nevis, and Skye. Many individual mountains in the Western Highlands have climbing potential and there are still discoveries to be made. Sea stacks and cliffs in the northern Isles have drawn climbers for many years, the Old Man of Hoy being one of the most famous.

As with walking, guides published by the Scottish Mountaineering Trust cover all the principal climbing areas.

# Downhill Skiing

There have been notable developments in the provision of winter sports facilities in Scotland in the past ten years. There are four main downhill ski centres, and the season runs from early December to Easter or later, if the snow holds. The main drawback has been, and will continue to be, the sheer unpredictability of the weather. Recent winters have seen excellent conditions in November, followed by a total thaw in January, then further snow cover lasting from March to June. Information on skiing prospects can be obtained from several sources – radio, TV and telephone – and many people resident in Scotland wait till the weekend before deciding whether or not to take off for the slopes.

*The Four Skiing Centres*

Scotland's main downhill ski area is based in Aviemore, in the Spey Valley. Once just a small village and rail halt, Aviemore has grown to a major holiday centre with year-round facilities and a number of large modern hotels.

The skiing is in the northern corries of the Cairngorm mountains and is served by a road rising to over 2,000 feet (600 m) at the two car parks. The lower of these is in Coire Cas, where chairlifts and tows take the skier up to 3,700 feet (1,120 m). Near the top is the Ptarmigan Restaurant, the highest in Britain, which seats only 48 people but a large 'day lodge' with a wide range of services has now been built at Coire Cas.

The more easterly corrie, Coire na Ciste, also has tows reaching up to 3,600 feet (1,100 m), giving the skier a run with a drop of over 1,300 feet (400 m) back to the car park. There are fewer facilities here, but the skiing is just as good.

A proposed major development westwards to the area known as Lurcher's Gully was rejected by the Secretary of State for Scotland in 1983 on environmental grounds.

The second centre, though called Glenshee, is in fact some way north of that glen. It centres round Cairnwell and Carn Aosda, two hills of just over 3,000 feet (about 915 m) on the west of the Perth-Braemar road (A93), which at that point rises to 2,100 feet (nearly 640 m). There are tows on both hills and also on Meall Odhar (Sunny Slope) on the east side of the road. A large café and shop offer shelter and refreshments. There is no accommodation near the slopes, and visiting skiers stay in Glenshee, Kirkmichael, Braemar or Blairgowrie. Glenshee hosts a Snow Fun Week each March with competitions for all the family.

The ski tow at Glencoe is one of the longest-established in Scotland, and the area is well loved and well used by weekend skiers, particularly from Glasgow. In keeping with the magnificent surroundings, the development is low key, essentially providing uplift for skiing with adequate, but not elaborate facilities. The skiing area, called the White Corries, is on Meall a'Bhuiridh, a mountain south of the A82 road and at the head of Glen Etive rather than Glencoe. The chairlift goes up to 2,000 feet (600 m), above which tows take skiers nearly to the mountain's summit. In the right conditions, the skiing is as good as any in Scotland, especially for experienced downhill skiers who can tackle the longer runs.

The fourth ski centre is at the Lecht, another point where an A-class road reaches over 2,000 feet (600 m), in this case between Deeside and Tomintoul. This road always used to be one of the first to get blocked by winter snows, but with the coming of the ski facilities it is kept clear these days in all but the very worst conditions. The skiing is aimed at families and beginners, rather than experts.

There has been considerable discussion on the future of skiing in Scotland, and a report has recently been prepared to indicate the areas most suitable for further development. These include the Drumochter hills south of Aviemore, Ben Wyvis and Aonach Mor (Spean Valley).

There are 12 dry ski slopes in Scotland, including Hillend, south of Edinburgh, at over 1,300 feet (400 m) the longest of any; it stages dry ski championships each year. Some of these slopes are open all year and would enable you to try a little skiing practice even in summer. There are dry ski slopes at Aberdeen (Bridge of Dee), Aviemore, Dundee, Edinburgh (Hillend), Glasgow (Bellahouston and Bearsden), Glenrothes, Glenshee, Jedburgh, Newmills (Ayrshire) and Polmont.

The Scottish Tourist Board's leaflet *Winter Sports in Scotland* provides full information on facilities, and gives addresses for the ski centres. Weather information can be obtained daily from the Scottish newspapers; by telephoning Dial-a-Ski on 031-246 8041 (1 December to 30 April); or by listening to regular radio and TV news bulletins.

# Ski Touring

Nordic, or cross-country, ski touring is becoming very popular in Scotland. Its advantage, once you are competent, is that you need no uplift facilities and can ski anywhere where there is snow. Basic techniques can be learnt in a few days. The skis and boots are lighter than those used for downhill skiing, and anyone with good balance should be able to pick up the 'gliding' or 'langlauf' step on their first day.

Ski touring is an excellent winter activity for walkers and backpackers, and has been further helped by the development of waxless skis. They will not give you such a fast ride as properly waxed skis, but they save the beginner having to learn all the intricacies of waxing.

Ski-touring courses can be found at several centres, notably around Aviemore. It is hoped that with the co-operation of the Forestry Commission, laid-out trails can be developed in a number of Scottish forests, and this has already started to happen in the Queen's Forest, near Aviemore.

# Shooting and Stalking

Deer and game birds have been shot for sport – and for food – on Scottish estates for many years. The pursuit of the two principal quarries – red deer and grouse – attracts sportsmen from many overseas countries, and the income from the 'let' of guns is vital to the economics of many estates. These activities are an integral part of the countryside scene in Scotland, and visitors should be aware of them and of the need to co-operate by not disturbing arrangements for shooting or stalking.

Shooting and stalking are at their height in the period between 12 August (the 'Glorious Twelfth', when the grouse season officially opens) and late

October, when the season for stags ends. Shooting does of course go on outside this period – pheasant, partridge and woodcock can be shot up to the end of January, for instance – but this is less likely to conflict with the visitor's desire to explore the countryside.

Let us start with deer. Red deer stags may be stalked at any time from 1 July to 20 October, and hinds from 20 October to 16 February. The main season for sporting guns is the autumn. The number of beasts to be shot should be controlled, both to give the best sport and to 'cull' the herd effectively so that numbers are not too high during the hard winter months. Otherwise deer can die from starvation, if there is insufficient food for the number of beasts on the ground.

The stalker's job is highly skilled and arduous. He has to know his 'beat' intimately so that he can take his clients where they are most likely to find their quarry; he must also be aware of the number of deer in his area, and thus the number by which the herd should be reduced to ensure a healthy surviving stock the following spring.

Stalking, in its roughest form, is a tough sport. The stalkers can be out all day, in all weathers, on foot, covering many miles before getting into position for a good shot at a stag. In recent years, tracked vehicles have come into use in some areas to get guns out to the likely areas more rapidly. As well as the traditional 'prize' of the antlers for the hunter, deer are an important source of income through the sale of venison, a meat which we can expect to grow in popularity in future years as more deer 'farms' are established.

It will be apparent that a stalk could be affected by a walker appearing on the scene and disturbing the deer. In the season, therefore, it is prudent to make local enquiries as to where stalking might be taking place before venturing on to the hills. Some areas, such as those owned by the National Trust for Scotland, are free from such restrictions. Stalking does not normally take place on Sundays, but on those days it would still be quite possible for walkers to move deer it was planned to stalk on the Monday.

Whereas the hunter pursues his stag, the grouse is driven to the gun by 'beaters' travelling in line across country. The guns are sited at 'butts' – small stone or turf shelters that you can find in many parts of the country. Here again, the birds could be driven in the wrong direction by walkers. If you come across a shooting party, polite enquiry will give you the information as to where you can walk without disturbing their day's sport.

Grouse are not the only birds to be shot; pheasant, capercaillie, snipe, partridge and woodcock are among the others. Some of these, including pheasant, are bred for the gun, and the quality of the sport can depend very much on the weather conditions the previous spring and on how much food the birds have had available in the intervening months. A cold, wet spring such as we had in 1983 does not encourage good growth of young heather and is liable to lead to a poor crop of game birds.

A good number of hotels in Scotland cater for the shooting clientele; they are listed in the Scottish Tourist Board's excellent leaflet *Shooting and Stalking in Scotland*. Hotels should always be contacted in advance to check what sporting arrangements they have, in order to avoid disappointment.

Under the provisions of the 1968 Firearms Act, anyone owning or using a rifle or shotgun must have a valid certificate. The firearms certificate (for rifles) costs £16 and the shotgun certificate £7, and both are valid for three years. Enquire at police stations in your area of residence. Visitors from overseas can either obtain a certificate in advance, or can bring a shotgun into the country without a licence providing that the visit lasts no longer than 30 days in any one year. Game licences must also be obtained in advance; prices range from £2 for the 'occasional' licence to £6 for a full year's use, and the licences can be obtained from post offices.

# Fishing

It is hardly surprising that fishing is one of the most popular recreations in Scotland. With 4,000 miles (6,400 km) of coastline, dozens of superb inland lochs, and a tremendous selection of salmon and trout rivers, it offers sport that could not be bettered anywhere in the world. Before describing the main types of fishing available, it might be of interest to look at the angler's prey, which in Scottish waters are principally the salmon, sea trout and brown trout. How do they develop?

Salmon and sea trout are migratory – that is, they spend some part of their life in the sea, but return to rivers to spawn. Salmon live the first two or three years of their life in the river where they were born. When they are ready to travel, the young fish – at this stage silvery in colour and known as smolts – swim downstream in shoals. In the open sea they feed and grow rapidly; Scottish salmon are known to travel as far as Greenland.

They may return to spawn after one, two or three years. Now known as grilse, they return to the river of their birth; it is still not known for certain how they achieve this remarkable piece of navigation, crossing hundreds of miles of open ocean and finding the correct river, then fighting their way up it to the spawning grounds.

Spawning exhausts the salmon. Most of the males die on the way downstream (if they are not caught). Most of the female fish reach the sea, but very few of them (less than 10 per cent) will make that upstream journey a second time.

Sea trout travel less far, feeding mainly in coastal waters, and they make many journeys from sea to river and back during their lifetime. Brown trout do not migrate, staying in the lochs and streams where they were born for their lifetime.

*Game Fishing*

Salmon and trout can be fished in very many Scottish waters, from the magnificent Tweed basin in the Borders up to the northern Highlands. The Borders rivers are rightly renowned, and the sport on the Tweed, Teviot, Till and other rivers is first class. A large number of 'beats' are available to the visiting angler, at very reasonable charges. Some hotels also offer special fishing holiday rates, and there are competitions for those that way inclined. As well as the species already mentioned, rainbow trout can be fished on some lochs.

The pattern is repeated as you travel further north, particularly in the fast-running rivers of the western seaboard. The season commonly extends from March to October. There is good fishing on many lochs, with boats available for hire locally. Loch fishing can be quite idyllic, with the sun shining and the gentle lap of water on the gunwales as you cast; or it can be very hard work, with the wind whipping up the waves as you crouch in your oilskins, trying to keep the boat afloat! Whatever the weather, the many fine hotels of the area will house and feed you in comfort.

*Coarse Fishing*

There is a good variety of coarse fish in Scottish waters – grayling, perch, roach, bream and carp among them. Pike feature too, the record being a monster of 32 lbs (14.5 kg) caught in Loch Lomond in 1977. There are many competitions, and an equal number of opportunities for quiet fishing on unfrequented beats. The season is again commonly March to October, although it can extend longer in some areas.

*Sea Angling*

This is a book about the countryside, not the sea, but it is worth mentioning that excellent sea angling is available all round the Scottish coast. The inner islands such as Arran, Mull and Skye offer good opportunities for the more adventurous angler, and such species as skate, pollack and dogfish can be fished, often using the trace or paternoster method.

The most popular area is probably the Clyde estuary and the Ayrshire coast, and competitions are again arranged here on a regular basis. For the really adventurous, there is great potential in Orkney and Shetland. The European Sea Angling Championships have twice been held on the island of Lewis and blue shark up to 85 lb (38.5 kg) have been landed in this area. 'Century' skate of 100 lb (45 kg) weight are not uncommon in Orkney waters and in 1978 a halibut of 224 lb (101.5 kg) was landed in Pentland waters.

*Fishing for the Disabled*

There are special facilities for disabled anglers in several places in Scotland – on the Tweed, at Lake of Menteith and at Lochore Meadows Country Park in Fife, for example. So far, the provision is mainly for loch fishing, with specially adapted boats, but some riverside sites with platform extensions have been created. The Committee for the Promotion of Angling for the Disabled (18/19 Claremont Crescent, Edinburgh EH7 4QD) will help with more detailed information.

*General Information*

The Scottish Tourist Board booklet *Scotland for Fishing* and a similar publication *Angling in the Scottish Borders* from the Scottish Borders Tourist Board give a mass of information. The Scottish Sports Council, 1 St Colme Street, Edinburgh EH3 6AA, will advise on courses.

# Orienteering

Competitive orienteering has been part of the sporting scene in Scotland for over twenty years; indeed, the first properly-run event in Britain was held near Dunkeld in 1962. It bore the grand name of the First Scottish Orienteering Championships, and the first nine places were taken by the nine Swedes who had come over from Stockholm to encourage the new sport!

Since then the 'forest sport' of map-reading and route choice has remained popular, with a full calendar of events each year. The British Orienteering Federation, in co-operation with the Forestry Commission, has established a number of non-competitive permanent 'wayfaring' courses where members of the public can try a simplified form of orienteering, using fixed marker posts. At the time of writing there were five such courses laid out in Scotland, as follows:

Achray Forest, Trossachs. GR 518028. Information pack from David Marshall Lodge, Aberfoyle, or Forestry Commission District Office, Ballanton, Aberfoyle.

Glentress Forest, 2 miles/3 km east of Peebles. GR 284398. Information pack from Glentress forest office or tourist information centre, High Street, Peebles.

Kirkhill Forest, near Aberdeen. Information pack from Forestry Commission, 6 Queen's Gate, Aberdeen, or Mr W. Robertson, 54 Auchmill Road, Bucksburn.

Queen's Forest, Aviemore. GR 979092. Information pack from forest office, Glenmore or campsite warden, Glenmore.

Torrieston Forest, Moray. GR 166588. Information pack from forest office, Newton Nursery, Elgin; tourist information office, Elgin; or Mr A. Sim, Torrieston.

There are also courses in non-Forestry Commission forests. For further information on these and on orienteering generally, write to British Orienteering Federation, 41 Dale Road, Matlock, Derbyshire DE4 3LT.

# Water Sports

There are opportunities for water sports on many Scottish lochs; sailing, canoeing and windsurfing are all available. The booklets *Boats and Yachts in Scotland* (Scottish Tourist Board) and *Yachting, Boating and Cruising* (HIDB) give further information. The Scottish Sports Council offers courses in sailing at its Glenmore Lodge and Cumbrae outdoor centres; Cumbrae has facilities for disabled sailors. The SYHA run courses in both sailing and canoeing.

The exciting sport of windsurfing can be sampled at the Lochearnhead Watersports Centre in Perthshire and Loch Insh Sailing School, Kincraig.

Boat trips for visitors, ranging from cruises on Loch Lomond to trips out with fishing vessels, are widely available. Check locally for details or enquire through area tourist boards.

# Other Activities

You can try almost anything in Scotland if you've a mind to. The Scottish Sports Council issue 'fact sheets' for all sports, and will be glad to supply further information. As a few examples, there are gliding courses at Portmoak, near Kinross in Tayside; hang gliding at the Cairnwell; diving at a number of places on the coast; and of course pony-trekking, a very well-established holiday pursuit and one on which information is available from the main tourist organisations.

# Youth Hostelling

The Scottish Youth Hostels Association was formed in 1931. The first hostel, at Broadmeadows, near Selkirk in the Border country, was opened in May of that year and is still welcoming travellers today. By the end of 1931 there were nine hostels in operation; today the network has grown to 80, covering the whole of mainland Scotland and reaching out to the northern and western islands.

Hostels today are as varied in character as the people who use them. There could hardly be a greater contrast than the hostels at Pitlochry – a former hotel, still very well appointed, with showers in every dormitory,

*Five Sisters of Kintail, Wester Ross, Highland*

and only opened in 1981 – and those at Loch Ossian or Craig, small buildings with spartan 'facilities', but offering a true welcome to the walker or cyclist who penetrates wild country to reach them.

The SYHA's aims remain the same as they were fifty years ago – 'to help all, but especially young people of limited means living and working in industrial and other areas to know, use and appreciate the Scottish countryside and places of historic and cultural interest in Scotland, and to promote their health, recreation, and education, particularly by providing simple hostel accommodation for them on their travels'. Pitlochry could hardly be called simple, but it is good to see the more remote hostels staying open and being well patronised in their short summer season.

There are in fact four grades of hostel, Grade 1 being the highest and Grade 4 the lowest. Hostel charges are still very moderate, and for a few pounds a night you can enjoy a comfortable bed, the company of like-minded people and at some hostels a good satisfying meal. Membership is open to all, and children over 5 years old can join their parents on a family membership card. There is an increasing, and welcome, trend for hostels to provide family rooms so that small children need not be separated from their parents.

All hostels are supervised by wardens, but the tradition is for hostellers to help with cleaning and tidying in order to keep costs down. Each morning the warden will allocate you a small 'duty' which you must do before you leave.

The SYHA now has about 50,000 members and welcomes many visitors from the rest of the United Kingdom and from overseas to its hostels each year. The importance of the hostel network as a means of enabling people to travel without incurring large bills for accommodation has been well recognised in recent years by the provision of grants through the Highlands and Islands Development Board, the Countryside Commission for Scotland and the Scottish Education Department for new hostel buildings and for renovating older ones.

The SYHA organises a number of activity holiday programmes each year. Ski schools are based on the hostels at Loch Morlich (Cairngorms) and Glenisla (Glenshee). During the summer a dozen or so hostels become bases for pony-trekking, hill walking, canoeing, climbing, sailing and multi-sport holidays. Full details of these holidays and of membership are available from the Scottish Youth Hostels Association, 7 Glebe Crescent, Stirling FK8 2JA.

# Camping and Caravanning

The trend towards self-catering holidays, which serve the dual purpose of saving money and giving the holiday-maker greater mobility, has not gone unnoticed in Scotland. Good camp and caravan sites are to be found everywhere from the Borders to Caithness and on the islands, although sites are fewer in number in the more remote areas.

Sites may be privately owned, run by local authorities, or developed by such bodies as the Forestry Commission. The Commission also has a number of chalet developments, all situated in fine scenic areas.

The touring caravanner is well provided for, with large sites in all the main scenic areas, and reasonable overnight charges, varying according to the facilities available. Nearly all sites have a well-stocked shop and many have a launderette, games room and play area for children. Many sites, too, will be happy to advise on recreational facilities nearby, such as fishing or hill walking, and the shop may well have local guidebooks and general tourist information on sale or for free distribution.

If your preference is for a static van, there is again plenty of choice. Booking in this case is by the week or fortnight, and charges can start as low as £25 for a farm site with only one or two vans. These are usually located by enquiry at the principal tourist information centre in the area; the larger sites are listed in the various guidebooks and their charges will be somewhat higher, as you would expect with the greater range of facilities provided.

Many of the sites catering for the touring caravanner also have pitches for motor vans, at similar charges. Drivers of both motor and towed vans should note that although there are many lay-bys on Scotland's A-class roads suitable for a stop for lunch or for a tea break, overnight stay in these lay-bys is not normally allowed. If you find yourself in an area where there is no proper site, local enquiry will usually solve the problem by locating an informal pitch.

It should also be noted that although road standards have improved greatly in recent years, quite a number of A roads are still single-lane with passing places. It is much appreciated by other drivers if vans pull off to let cars and commercial traffic pass. If you are on holiday, you should not be in any great hurry, and your courtesy will improve everyone's temper.

The holidaymaker with a tent, be it large or small, will also find plenty of good sites in Scotland. Guides should be studied with care, for some of the large caravan sites do not take tents, all their pitches being allocated for vans. You are unlikely to have to travel far to find a tent site in such instances; the lightweight camper is particularly well off in such a spacious country and is unlikely to be refused permission to camp.

There is of course wonderful scope for 'wild' camping, and I have enjoyed some memorable nights pitched high on the hillside, surrounded by space and with the silence only broken by the chuckling of a burn beside me. It is appreciated if you ask permission to camp wherever you are, but if you are really in the wild this simply may not be possible. The freedom of access which applies to the walker also of course applies to the backpacker, and the only code is *always* to leave your campsite in immaculate condition, so that no one would know you have been there. With good lightweight stoves readily available, there is no need to light a fire, and indeed it may well be dangerous to do so, with a high fire risk at many times of the year.

As with other recreations, the camper or caravanner will find sites emptier in the spring or autumn. In high season, advance booking may be essential and for those who are tied to school holidays the essential reading is *Camping and Caravan Sites*, published by the Scottish Tourist Board. It lists about 350 sites and gives all the details you need. Members of the Camping Club and the Caravan Club will have their own site guides; both clubs have sites in Scotland which their members can use.

Joining a club can be useful in many ways. Their expertise, built up probably over many years, is at your disposal. Lots of them run weekend 'rallies' where you can meet other club members and undoubtedly learn a lot as well as enjoying yourself.

Scotland, with its superb scenery and space to breathe, is in many ways an ideal country for a camping or caravanning holiday, and I have no doubt that this side of the leisure market will continue to increase over the next decade.

# TOURISM

The structure of tourism in Scotland has undergone considerable changes in the recent past. Until 1 April 1983, tourism was in the charge of the regional councils; after that date, as the result of a far-reaching report, the responsibility was largely devolved to district councils.

In practice, this has meant that in the eight mainland regions excluding Highland, Area Tourist Boards have been set up to serve their particular district. It is believed that these boards, because they serve smaller areas and also have considerable input directly from the trade, will be more effective than the larger regional tourist departments they have replaced.

Highland Region was an exception in that, under the joint aegis of the regional council and the Highlands and Islands Development Board, 15 Area Tourist Organisations were already in operation, and working very well. These ATOs have in part served as the model for the way the newer ATBs have been set up.

Another difference is that the ATBs come under the overall guidance of the national body, the Scottish Tourist Board. The Highland and Island ATOs report to the HIDB. It is possible that in the near future there will be a further change, with all these bodies taking the same name – probably Area Tourist Board—and all of them reporting to the STB. A further development has been the establishment of a Confederation of Scottish Tourism as a powerful 'lobbying' body to represent the tourism view to local and national government.

As with any scheme of this magnitude, there are exceptions to the general rule. Two regions – Borders and Dumfries and Galloway – have decided to operate as regional tourist boards and not divide into districts, and three districts – Moray, Kirkcaldy and Edinburgh – at the time of writing had not felt it necessary to set up Area Tourist Boards, preferring to continue with the district councils exercising the responsibility for tourism. This makes a total as I write of 36 ATBs and ATOs, and three tourism departments of district councils. They are listed on page 76, and all of them will be more than pleased to supply the visitor with helpful information.

The 'sharp end' of tourism is where the contact – often the vital first contact – takes place, and most frequently that is at tourist information centres. Scotland is very well equipped with tourist information centres, having about 150 of them in the summer season. They vary from caravans to quite large buildings; some, such as that at Bannockburn near Stirling, were specially built for the job. Most tourist information centres are open from Easter or early May until October, although a few, mostly in the cities, stay open all the year. A free booklet, entitled *Tourist Information Centres,* giving full addresses, telephone numbers, opening times and other information, is available from the Scottish Tourist Board.

The services offered by the tourist information centres are similar whatever their size. They can all advise on accommodation, booking you ahead if you wish (there is a small charge for this service, but it is a comfort to know that you have a bed reserved). They can tell you about local attractions, the availability of such things as fishing and sailing, and offer a good range of guides, bus and rail timetables, and other helpful literature. They are there to serve you and the more use you make of them, the happier they are.

In many areas you will nowadays find hotels grouping together to offer services and accommodation to the visitor, sharing the cost of promotional literature. The new set-up encourages this kind of initiative and there is no doubt that the visitor benefits.

Tourism is a very important industry for Scotland. In some places in recent years it has been virtually the *only* business with potential for expansion. It has another vital function in providing employment for local people. The new Area Tourist Boards and their longer-established sister bodies in the Highlands and Islands will be working hard to realise the potential that they know still exists. That means improving standards in hotels, offering the visitor better facilities, making a strong push with such promotions as the successful *Taste of Scotland*, in which hotels and restaurants offered Scottish dishes, and researching their potential markets much more closely. Particular market 'sectors' such as fishermen, hill walkers, or simply sun-seekers will find themselves lured by special offers.

All this is to the good, as long as development is kept under control. The publications of the various tourist boards, as well as those of the STB itself, will in future undoubtedly contain more in the way of special interest or activity holidays, family breaks, and off-season reductions, to lengthen the season and show even more people what Scotland has to offer.

# PART II
# GAZETTEER

# INTRODUCTION TO THE GAZETTEER

The gazetteer is divided into regions, and listings for each region are divided into a number of categories (castles, historic buildings, nature reserves and so on). Notes on these categories, how they are arranged, and where to get further information are given below.

The addresses listed under General Information will be useful in gathering material before your trip. The Scottish Tourist Board in particular have a large range of very useful publications, some of which are free. Area Tourist Boards and Organisations are always happy to supply literature and information on their 'patch': their boundaries are shown on the map.

We do not pretend that this gazetteer is completely exhaustive, but we have tried to include as much useful information as we can. Opening times and facilities do tend to change from year to year, and the author and publishers will be glad to receive a note of any alterations found by users of this book so that they can be included in future editions. While we have taken every care in the compilation of this information we can take no responsibility for any errors or inaccuracies, however caused.

## General Information

Scottish Tourist Board, 23 Ravelston Terrace, Edinburgh EH4 3EU (031-332 2433)

Countryside Commission for Scotland, Battleby, Redgorton, Perth PH1 3EW (0738 27921)

Forestry Commission, Information Branch, 231 Corstorphine Road, Edinburgh EH12 7AT (031-334 0303)

Highlands and Islands Development Board, Bridge House, Bank Street, Inverness IV1 1QR (0463 234171)

National Trust for Scotland, 5 Charlotte Square, Edinburgh EH2 4DU (031-226 5922)

Nature Conservancy Council, Scottish Office, 12 Hope Terrace, Edinburgh EH9 2AS (031-447 4784)

Royal Society for the Protection of Birds, Scottish Office, 17 Regent Terrace, Edinburgh EH7 5BN (031-556 5624)

Scottish Sports Council, 1 St Colme Street, Edinburgh EH3 6AA (031-225 8411)

Scottish Wildlife Trust, 25 Johnston Terrace, Edinburgh EH1 2NH (031-226 4602)

Scottish Youth Hostels Association, 7 Glebe Crescent, Stirling FK8 2JA (0786 2821)


## Area Tourist Boards

Aviemore & Spey Valley T.B., Grampian Road, Aviemore PH22 1PP (0479 810454)

Ayrshire & Burns Country T.B., 39 Sandgate, Ayr KA7 1BG (0292 284196)

Ayrshire & Clyde Coast T.B., Cunninghame House, Irvine, Ayrshire KA12 8EE (0294 74166)

Ayrshire Valleys T.B., P.O. Box 13, Civic Centre, Kilmarnock KA1 1BY (0563 21140)

Banff & Buchan T.B., Collie Lodge, Banff AB4 1AU (02612 2789)

Caithness T.B., Whitechapel Road, Wick KW1 4EA (0955 2596)

City of Aberdeen T.B., St Nicholas House, Broad Street, Aberdeen AB9 1DE (0224 632727)

City of Dundee T.B., City Chambers, Dundee DD1 3BY (0382 23141)

City of Edinburgh District Council, Dept of Tourism, 9 Cockburn Street, Edinburgh EH1 1BR (031-226 6591)

Clyde Valley T.B., South Vennel, Lanark ML11 7JT

Dumfries & Galloway T.B., Douglas House, Newton Stewart, Wigtownshire DG8 6DQ (0671 2549)

Dunoon & Cowal T.B., Information Centre, Pier Esplanade, Dunoon PA23 7HL (0369 3755)

East Lothian T.B., Brunton Hall, Musselburgh EH21 6AF (031-665 3711)

Fort William & Lochaber T.B., Travel Centre, Fort William PH33 6AN (0397 3781)

Forth Valley T.B., Burgh Hall, The Cross, Linlithgow, West Lothian EH49 7AH (0506 843306)

Gordon District T.B., St Nicholas House, Broad Street, Aberdeen AB9 1DE (0224 632727)

Greater Glasgow T.B., City Chambers, George Square, Glasgow G2 1DU (041-221 5238)

Inverness, Loch Ness & Nairn T.B., 23 Church Street, Inverness IV1 1EZ (0463 234353)

Isle of Arran T.B., Information Centre, The Pier, Brodick, Isle of Arran KA27 8AU (0770 2140/2401)

Isle of Skye and South West Ross T.B., Tourist Information Centre, Portree, Isle of Skye IV51 9BZ (0478 2137)

Kincardine & Deeside T.B., 45 Station Road, Banchory AB3 3XX (03302 2066)

Loch Lomond, Stirling & Trossachs T.B., Beechwood House, St Ninians Road, Stirling FK8 2HU (0786 70945)

Mid Argyll, Kintyre & Islay T.B., The Pier, Campbeltown, Argyll PA28 6EF (0586 52056)

Oban, Mull & District T.B., Boswell House, Argyll Square, Oban PA34 4AN (0631 63122)

Orkney T.B., Information Centre, Broad Street, Kirkwall, Orkney KW15 1DH (0856 2856)

Outer Hebrides T.B., 4 South Beach Street, Stornoway, Isle of Lewis PA87 2XY (0851 3088)

Perthshire T.B., P.O. Box 33, George Inn Lane, Perth PH1 5LG (0738 27958)

Ross & Cromarty T.B., Information Centre, North Kessock, Inverness IV1 1XB (0463 73505)

Rothesay & Isle of Bute T.B., The Pier, Rothesay, Isle of Bute PA20 9AQ (0700 2151)

St Andrews & North-East Fife T.B., 2 Queens Gardens, St Andrews, Fife KY16 9TE (0334 74609)

Scottish Borders T.B., Municipal Buildings, High Street, Selkirk TD7 4JX (0750 20555)

Shetland T.B., Information Centre, Market Cross, Lerwick, Shetland ZE1 0LU (0595 3434)

Sutherland T.B., The Square, Dornoch, Sutherland IV25 3SD (0862 810400)

# The Gazetteer Categories

*Antiquities*

Anything from pre-medieval times is included here. Many of the entries are marked AM to indicate that they are scheduled Ancient Monuments in the care of the Secretary of State for Scotland (which in practice means the Ancient Monuments Division). These monuments have two types of opening times – standard times, marked 'std', which is as follows:

| October-March: | Monday-Saturday | 09.30-16.00 |
| | Sunday | 14.00-16.00 |
| April-September: | Monday-Saturday | 09.30-19.00 |
| | Sunday | 14.00-19.00 |

or open at all reasonable times, marked 'art'. The latter type of opening usually applies to monuments for which there is no admission charge, often because they are ruins rather than complete buildings or sites.

Many of the monuments listed have guidebooks or leaflets written about them, which are inexpensive and give a lot of information. These are available on site or at tourist information centres.

*Castles*

The castles listed range from gaunt ruins to magnificent fortified houses, some still lived in and superbly well preserved, either by their owners (as, for example, Blair or Cawdor) or by bodies such as the National Trust for Scotland (as with the castles of Mar). For those which are scheduled Ancient Monuments, the same notes apply as for Antiquities. For the others, opening times have been given where known. Fortified and pele towers, notably in the Borders, have been included in this category. Castles in towns and cities such as the famous strongholds at Edinburgh and Stirling are outside the scope of this book, but are of course well worth visiting.

### Country Parks

There are 28 country parks at present in Scotland, many of them quite close to large areas of population, giving opportunities for recreation of various kinds. They are open all year and many have a ranger service operating. Further information on country parks is available from the Countryside Commission for Scotland (and see also pages 47-54).

### Gardens

Only gardens which are open regularly have been included in this list. Many other gardens open occasionally, and when they do are well worth seeing. For details see local or national press (usually on Saturdays) or the booklet *Scotland's Gardens*, published by the Scotland's Gardens Scheme, 26 Castle Terrace, Edinburgh EH1 2EL.

### Historic Buildings and Monuments

This section includes the great houses which are not listed as castles – for example, Falkland Palace – and monuments of particular interest which do not qualify for the Antiquities section.

### Industry

The range in this section is quite surprising, covering everything from nuclear power plants to perfume bottling! In general the entries are self-explanatory, but a word of advice on two of the particular categories might be helpful.

*Distilleries* usually stop the production of whisky for a month or so in July and August (the 'silent season') in order to carry out essential maintenance of equipment and machinery. Many still accept visitors during this period, but you might not see the full production process. Where distilleries prefer visitors to book in advance, this is indicated in the entry.

*Lighthouses* listed here are normally open to visitors between 14.00 and one hour before sunset, but as there are times when you cannot visit them (for example, when essential maintenance is being carried out), you should always try to telephone in advance. For this reason, lighthouses are listed simply by their location and the telephone number is given.

I have not attempted to list craft workshops (potters, jewellers, leatherworkers, weavers, horncraft, etc.) as a rough check indicated that there were something like 1,300 of them in Scotland and I felt this was a task somewhat beyond me! *Directory of Scottish Crafts and Craftsmen*, published by the Scottish Development Agency (Rosebery House, Haymarket Terrace, Edinburgh EH12 5EZ), gives details of many of these workshops: area tourist boards will supply further information.

## Museums

Museums with relevance to the countryside or in country locations have been included in this section. The STB guide, *Museums and Galleries in Scotland*, published in collaboration with the Council for Museums and Galleries in Scotland, gives comprehensive coverage.

## Nature Reserves

At the time of compiling this section, there were just under 150 nature reserves in Scotland. Of these, 62 were National Nature Reserves (NNRs), established by the Nature Conservancy Council as sites of national importance for study and research into nature conservation. The Scottish Wildlife Trust owns or manages 58 reserves and the Royal Society for the Protection of Birds has 23. Many of these reserves have restricted access, and only those with free access or with facilities for receiving visitors are listed. Full lists of reserves can be obtained from the following:

Nature Conservancy Council, 12 Hope Terrace, Edinburgh EH9 2AS (Information Sheet no. 4: National Nature Reserves in Scotland).

Royal Society for the Protection of Birds, 17 Regent Terrace, Edinburgh EH7 5BN (Reserves visiting leaflet).

Scottish Wildlife Trust, 25 Johnston Terrace, Edinburgh EH1 2NH.

National Trust for Scotland, 5 Charlotte Square, Edinburgh EH2 4DU.

## Religious Houses

This section lists churches, cathedrals, abbeys and the like, excluding those in large towns and cities. Some of them are scheduled Ancient Monuments.

The listings here are of centres either with a particular theme – forestry, for example – or those designed to offer the visitor a full information service, such as the Heritage Centre at Bannockburn, near Stirling. There are smaller visitor or information centres at other places, such as country parks and National Trust properties.

*Walking*

The scope for walking is Scotland is vast, as is explained earlier in the book (page 55). This section lists the few waymarked long-distance paths in Scotland and other walks specifically designed for the visitor. Many of these are *forest walks*, for which further information can be obtained from the Forestry Commission – either the Information Branch in Edinburgh or forest offices on site, when these are open.

Other walks listed include *nature trails*. Places such as country parks usually have a good footpath network. The STB booklets *Walks and Trails in Scotland* and *Hillwalking in Scotland* give further information and will be found helpful.

# Abbreviations

| | |
|---|---|
| AM | Ancient Monument |
| art | Open at all reasonable times |
| D | Provision of facilities for the disabled |
| G | Leaflet/guide available |
| NCC | Nature Conservancy Council |
| NNR | National Nature Reserve |
| NTS | National Trust for Scotland |
| P | Parking |
| R | Restaurant/tearoom |
| RSPB | Royal Society for the Protection of Birds |
| STB | Scottish Tourist Board |
| std | Open as detailed above (page 78) under Antiquities |
| SWT | Scottish Wildlife Trust |
| T | Toilets |

Numbers in parentheses such as (NX 222717) are Ordnance Survey map six-figure grid references.

# BORDERS

## Antiquities

**Edin's Hall Broch**   On north-east slope of Cockburn Law, 4 miles/7 km north of Duns. AM; art; free. Exceptionally large Iron Age broch. Access on foot only.

## Castles

**Ayton Castle**   A1, 5 miles/8 km north of Berwick. May-Sept, Wed, Sun and Bank Holidays: 14.00-17.00. A 19th-century sandstone building similar to Brodick Castle on Arran (both designed by J. G. Graham). Fine Victorian furniture and painted ceilings.

**Fast Castle**   Off A1107, 4 miles/7 km north-west of Coldingham. Art; free. Gaunt remains of a former stronghold of the Home family, set dramatically on the very edge of the sea. Access on foot only—*great care must be taken.*

**Floors Castle**   B6089, s miles/3 km north-west of Kelso. May-Sept, Mon-Thur and Sun: 11.30-17.30. Adam mansion built in 1721, home of the Duke of Roxburghe. Grounds and gardens also open.

**Greenknowe Tower**   A6105, ½ mile/1 km west of Gordon. AM; std; free. Late 16th-century fortified tower house held by the Seton family for generations.

**Hermitage Castle**   Off B6399, 16 miles/25 km north-east of Langholm. AM; std. A 13th-century fortress to which Mary Queen of Scots rode from Jedburgh in 1566 to meet Bothwell, a ride which nearly caused her death.

**Hume Castle**   B6364, 6 miles/10 km north of Kelso. Open all year, Mon-Sat: 10.00-17.00; Sun: 14.00-17.00 (key from Mrs Murray, The Smiddy). A 13th-century stronghold on a hill, 'restored' as a sham antique by Earl of Marchmont in the 1790s. Good views.

**Neidpath Castle**   A72, 1 mile/1½ km west of Peebles. Easter-Oct. Mon-Sat: 10.00-13.00, 14.00-18.00; Sun: 13.00-18.00. Fraser 'tower' perched high above the Tweed; three floors high, now in the care of Lord Wemyss.

**Newark Castle**   Off A708, 4 miles/7 km west of Selkirk. Free. For admission apply Buccleuch Estates, Bowhill. Five-storeyed oblong tower house, with arms of James I on gable. *Care needed.*

**Smailholm Tower**   Off B6404, 7 miles/11 km west of Kelso. AM; std; free. Outstanding example of pele tower, nearly 60 ft/19m high, saved from demolition by Sir Walter Scott.

**Thirlestane Castle**   In Lauder (A68). Open mid May-end June and Sept, Wed and Sun; Jul-Aug daily except Fri, 1400-1700. The largest of all Border castles, with splendid furniture and paintings. Combined admission charge with Border Country Life Museum.

# Historic Buildings and Monuments

**Abbotsford**   B6360, 2 miles/3 km west of Melrose. Apr-Oct, Mon-Sat: 10.00-17.00; Sun: 14.00-17.00. Home of Sir Walter Scott, with many mementoes of the writer and his life.

**Bemersyde**   B6356, 4 miles/7 km east of Melrose. Enquire locally. Home of the Haig family, including Earl Haig, leader of British Forces in the First World War.

**Bowhill**   A708, 1 mile/1½ km west of Selkirk. Easter, May-Sept, Mon, Wed, Thurs, Sat and Sun: 12.30-17.00; Jul-Aug daily, except Fri. Home of Duke of Buccleuch; it has many fine paintings, including one by Leonardo da Vinci, rare clocks and extensive grounds.

**Carolside**   A68, 3 miles/5 km north of Melrose. Jun-Aug: garden Wed and Sat: 14.00-17.00, house by arrangement tel. Earlston 272. Adam style house with notable collection of roses and herb garden.

**James Hogg Monument**   Ettrick, 1 mile/1½ km west of B7009. Art; free. On the site of the birthplace of the 'Ettrick Shepherd', who is buried in the graveyard of the nearby church.

**Manderston**   A6105, 1½ miles/2½ km east of Duns. May-Sept, Sun and Thur: 14.00-17.30. Edwardian country house with fine domestic quarters to be seen. Grounds and garden.

**Mellerstain**   A6089, 3 miles/5 km south of Gordon. May-Sept, Sun-Fri: 12.30-16.30. Georgian mansion with superb paintings, Adam ceilings, fine gardens.

**Monteviot** Off A68, 3½ miles/6 km north of Jedburgh. May-Oct, Wed only: 13.30-17.30. Home of Marquess of Lothian, dating from mid-18th century. See also Lothian Estates Centre (p. 87).

**Traquair** B7062, 7 miles/11 km east of Peebles. Easter-Oct daily: 13.30-17.30 (Jul-Aug open 10.30). Oldest continually occupied house in Scotland, with brewhouse, craft workers and gardens.

# Industry

**Jedburgh Kiltmakers** Bankend North, Jedburgh. Apr-Oct daily: 09.00-17.00. Visitors can see how kilts and kilted skirts are made.

**Traquair House** Brewhouse where Traquair House Ale is made. See under Historic Buildings (above).

# Museums

**Borders Country Life Museum** Thirlestane Castle, Lauder, off A68. Apr-Oct, Mon-Fri: 10.00-17.00; Sat-Sun: 14.00-17.00; Nov-Mar, Mon-Fri: 10.00-17.00. Museum opened in 1982 to show rural and agricultural life in past times in the Borders. Demonstrations of farm practices and machinery.

**Jim Clark Memorial Room** 44 Newtown Street, Duns. Apr-Sept, Mon-Sat: 10.00-13.00 and 14.00-18.00; Sun: 14.00-18.00 only. Unique museum to former motor-racing champion whose home was Duns.

**Coldstream Museum** Market Square, Coldstream. Apr-Sept daily, except Mon, 14.00-17.00 (Sat: 10.00-13.00). Displays historical material associated with Coldstream Guards regiment and items of local history.

**Eyemouth Museum** The Auld Kirk, Eyemouth. Easter weekend, then May-mid-Oct, Mon-Sat: 10.00-18.00; Sun: 14.00-18.00. Museum portrays the history of the Eyemouth fishing industry, with particular reference to the disaster of 1881, in which 129 Eyemouth men were lost at sea. Museum is also the start of the Eyemouth Town Trail and incorporates tourist information centre.

**Hirsel Estate Information Centre** The Hirsel, 1 mile/1½ km west of Coldstream, on A697. Open all year, daily, daylight hours. Covers all aspects of the estate and history of the house and the Home family, who still live there (house not open). Free (donations invited).

**Scottish Museum of Wool Textiles**  In Walkerburn, on A72, 8 miles/13 km east of Peebles. All year, Mon-Fri: 10.00-17.00. Easter-end Sep, Sat: 11.00-16.00; Sun: 14.00-16.00. Part of Ballantyne's Tweedvale Mill with displays of tartans and patterns and demonstrations of spinning.

# Gardens

**Dawyck Arboretum**  B712, 8 miles/13 km south of Peebles. Easter-Sept, daily: 12.00-17.00. Rare trees, shrubs, woodland walks. Now an outstation of the Royal Botanic Garden, Edinburgh.

**The Hirsel**  A697, 1 mile/1½ km west of Coldstream. Open all year, daylight hours. Estate of Lord Home. Fine trees, nature walks, loch, information centre. Free (donations invited).

**Kailzie**  B7062, 3 miles/5 km east of Peebles. Apr-late Oct, daily: 11.00-17.30. Walled garden, wild garden, pheasantry, pond with water-fowl, woodland walks. Art gallery and shop.

**Manderston**  A6105, 2 miles/3 km east of Duns. Open 15 May-end Sept, Sun and Thurs plus bank holidays, and Mondays and Tuesdays during August: 14.00-17.30. Formal and woodland gardens noted for rhododendrons. House also open (see p. 83).

**Priorwood**  In Melrose, next to the Abbey. Apr, Nov and Dec, Mon-Fri: 10.00-13.00 and 14.00-17.30; Sat: 10.00-17.30; May-Oct, Mon-Sat: 10.00-18.00; Sun: 14.00-17.00. Small formal garden (NTS) specialising in flowers for drying. Shop. Free (donations invited).

# Nature Reserves

**Duns Castle** (SWT)  Off A6112, 1 mile/1 km north of Duns. By permit only from Mr W. Waddell, 26 The Mount, Duns.

**St Abb's Head** (SWT/NTS)  Parking at Northfield Farm, just off B6438 (no charge). Parking (charge) for elderly and disabled people near St Abb's lighthouse. Full-time ranger; leaflet. This headland with high rocky cliffs is famous for its breeding seabirds which include guillemots, razorbills, shags, fulmars and kittiwakes. Scrubland around a freshwater loch attracts numbers of migrant birds. The area was declared a NNR in October 1983.

**Yetholm Loch** (SWT)  Off B6352, turning to Lochtower. Breeding and winter wildfowl, interesting marsh plants. No facilities.

# Religious Houses

**Coldingham Priory**  A1107, 3 miles/5 km north-west of Eyemouth. Art; free. Benedictine Priory founded about 1100 by King Edgar; the choir has been restored and is used as the parish church.

**Dryburgh Abbey**  Off A68, 6 miles/10 km south of Melrose. AM; std. Border abbey founded by Hugh de Morville; cloisters are particularly fine. Sir Walter Scott is buried there.

**Edrom Norman Arch**  Off A6105, 3 miles/5 km east of Duns. AM; art; free. Norman chancel arch now standing behind the parish church.

**Fogo Church**  Off B6460, 3 miles/5 km south-west of Duns. Art; free. Features include an outside staircase giving access to the 'laird's loft', dating from 1670.

**Jedburgh Abbey**  A68, on south side of Jedburgh. AM; std. Superbly sited abbey by Jed Water; extensive remains include a fine rose window and carved Norman doorway.

**Lady Kirk**  B6470, 4 miles/7 km east of Swinton. Art; free. Church built by James IV in about 1500, as an offering of thanks for his escape from death by drowning in the Tweed.

**Melrose Abbey**  A72, Melrose. AM; std. Cistercian house dating from 1135, with splendid carvings including a pig playing the pipes. Priorwood Garden (NTS) is next door.

**Yarrow Kirk**  A708, 12 miles/19 km west of Selkirk. Church dates from 1640 and has associations with Sir Walter Scott, James Hogg (the 'Ettrick Shepherd' poet) and Wordsworth.

# Visitor Centres

**Abbey St Bathans Trout Farm**  Off B6355, 7 miles/11 km north of Duns. May-Sep daily: 11.00-17.00; Oct-Apr, Sat and Sun: 11.00-17.00 Interpretive centre with mural display of life in the area from prehistoric times to the present. Trout can be fed.

**John Buchan Centre**  South end of Broughton village, 4 miles/7 km east of Biggar. Easter-mid Oct daily: 14.00-17.00. Former church housing exhibition of the life and work of John Buchan (Lord Tweedsmuir), whose mother was born in Broughton.

**Lothian Estates Woodland Centre**  Harestanes, 3½ miles/6 km north of Jedburgh. Apr-Oct, Sun and Wed: 13.00-17.30; July-Aug, Sun-Thur: 13.00-17.30. Woodland walks, pinery, children's play area, outdoor board games, audio-visual programmes, tearoom. See also Monteviot (p. 84).

# Walking

**Long-distance Path**  The *Southern Upland Way*, stretching over 200 miles/320 km, from Portpatrick near Stranraer to the Berwickshire coast passes right across the Borders and was opened in April 1984. Further information from Countryside Commission for Scotland, Battleby, Redgorton, Perth.

**Eildon Hills Walk**  Details from Tourist Information Centre, Priorwood, Melrose. Hill and riverside walk of 5 miles/8 km. Waymarked, guidebook.

# Forest Walks

**Cardrona**  3½ miles/5½ km east of Peebles on B7062. Car park, picnic place, three walks (2 miles/3 km, 3 miles/5 km, 4½ miles/7 km).

**Craik**  Borthwick Water picnic place, go 5 miles/8 km west of Hawick on B711 to Roberton, then 8 miles/13 km south-west along Borthwick Water to Craik. Two walks (1½ miles/2½ km, 3 miles/5 km).

**Elibank and Traquair**  6 miles/10 km west of Galashiels on A707. One walk (1¼ miles/2 km).

**Glentress**  2 miles/3 km east of Peebles on A72. Car park, information centre, wayfaring course, toilets. Four walks (1 mile/1½ km, 2½ miles/ 4 km, 4 miles/7 km, 4½ miles/7½ km).

**Lammermuir**  Pease Bay Forest Walk, on minor road 2 miles/3 km east of Cockburnspath (A1).

*Gruinard Bay, Wester Ross, Highland*

# CENTRAL

## Antiquities

**Antonine Wall** (AM) This northerly outpost of the Roman empire stretched from Bo'ness to Old Kilpatrick on the Clyde. Built AD 138-43, it was a turf rampart with a ditch and fort every two miles (3 km). It can be seen off A803 east of Bonnybridge, and at Rough Castle (below).

**Rough Castle** (AM) Off B816, 6 miles/10 km west of Falkirk. The best preserved of the Antonine Wall forts. Open at all times; free.

## Castles

**Castle Campbell** Dollar Glen, off A91. AM; std. 15th-century stronghold with commanding views, burned by Cromwell's troops in the 1650s. Dollar Glen (NTS) makes a spectacular approach to the castle.

**Doune Castle** A84, 8 miles/13 km north of Stirling. Apr-Oct daily: 10.00-16.30 (to 17.00 Jun-Aug; closed Thur Apr and Oct). In the hands of the Earls of Moray for 400 years, these splendid ruins are well worth a visit.

**Menstrie Castle** A91, 5 miles/8 km east of Stirling. NTS. May-Sept, Wed, Sat and Sun: 14.30-17.00. Castle is now converted into flats; a 'commemoration room' displays the coats of arms of 107 baronetcies from Nova Scotia, Canada. Menstrie was the birthplace of Sir William Alexander, James VI's Lieutenant in the colony.

## Country Parks

**Gartmorn Dam** Off A908, 2 miles/3 km north-east of Alloa (170 acres/ 68 ha). Reservoir with good birdlife, visitor centre, nature trail, hides, picnic areas. Ranger.

**Muiravonside** A706, south-west of Linlithgow (150 acres/61 ha). River Avon, woodland walks, formal gardens. Ranger.

# Gardens

**Doune Park Gardens**   A84, 1½ miles/2½ km north of Doune. Apr-Oct daily: 10.00-17.00 (18.00 Jun-Aug). Extensive walled garden, pinetum, woodland walks.

**Gargunnock House**   A811, 6 miles/10 km north-west of Stirling. Apr-end Oct, Wed: 13.00-17.00. Small shrub and flower garden, woodland walk. House not open. Free (donations invited).

**Keir Gardens**   Off B824, 6 miles/10 km north of Stirling. Apr-Oct, Tue-Thur 14.00-18.00. Water garden, yew tree house, daffodils, borders.

# Industry

**Glengoyne Distillery**   A81, 3 miles/5 km north-west of Blanefield. Mar-Nov, Mon-Fri: tours at 10.00, 11.30 and 15.00. From mid-July to end Aug whisky is not produced, but distillery can still be visited (Glenfyne Distillery Co.).

# Monuments

**Wallace Monument**   Off A91, 2 miles/3 km north of Stirling. Daily, 10.00-17.00 (Feb and Oct), -18.00 (Mar and Sept), -19.00 (Apr and Aug), -20.00 (May-Jul). Commemorates William Wallace, who defeated the English at the battle of Stirling Bridge. Display of mementoes, including Wallace's sword. Fine views from top of tower, walks in surrounding woodland.

# Museums

**Doune Motor Museum**   A84, 1 mile/1½ km north of Doune village. Apr-Oct daily: 10.00-17.00. Large collection of vintage cars including a 1905 Rolls Royce, the second oldest in existence.

# Nature and Wildlife

**Blair Drummond Safari Park**   A84, 5 miles/8 km north of Stirling. Easter-end Oct daily: 10.00-18.00. Giraffes, camels, monkeys, etc. roaming free; tigers, lions, bears, etc. in large enclosures. Drive round or use Safari bus. Children's play area, pets corner. *D, P, R, T.*

**Dollar Glen** (NTS) Off A91 in Dollar. Spectacular wooded gorge with paths, bridges and waterfalls. Art; free.

## Religious Houses

**Balquhidder Church** Minor road off A84, 14 miles/22 km north of Callander. Church contains 8th-century St Angus' Stone and old Gaelic Bibles; Rob Roy Macgregor, his wife and two of his sons are buried in the churchyard.

**Cambuskenneth Abbey** Off A91, 2 miles/3 km east of Stirling (1 mile/1½ km walk from Stirling). AM; std; closed winter months. Augustinian house founded in 1147; scene of Robert Bruce's Parliament in 1326.

**Inchmahome Priory** On an island in the Lake of Menteith, off A81, 4 miles/7 km east of Aberfoyle. Ferry operates Apr-Sept: 09.30-19.00. AM. Ruins of an Augustinian house founded in 1238. Mary Queen of Scots came here as an infant. The lake has very fine birdlife.

## Visitor Centres

**Bannockburn Heritage Centre** A9, 3 miles/5 km south of Stirling. Mar-Oct, daily: 10.00-18.00. Exhibition, audio-visual programme, tourist information centre (NTS/STB).

**David Marshall Lodge** A821, 1 mile/1½ km north of Aberfoyle. Mid-Mar-mid-Oct daily: 11.00-19.00. Forestry Commission exhibition of forestry and Trossachs associations. Walks, nature trail.

## Walking

Stirling District Council issue leaflets on walking routes in the area.

**Long-distance Path** The West Highland Way passes through the region on its way from Glasgow to Fort William (Blanefield – Drymen – Balmaha – Loch Lomondside – Crianlarich – Tyndrum – Bridge of Orchy). Details from the Countryside Commission for Scotland.

**Devon Way** Part of an old railway line by the River Devon has been converted into a footpath. Access at or near Tillicoultry, Dollar, Pool of Muckhart.

# Forest Walks

**Achray** David Marshall Lodge, Aberfoyle. Visitor centre, exhibition, toilets, refreshments. Provision for disabled. Waterfall trail – short walk with interpretative panels. Maps of longer walking routes available at Lodge.

**Ben A'an** (1,520 feet/500 m). A821, 6 miles 10 km north of Aberfoyle. Steep walk of 1½ miles/2½ km, good views, rocky in places.

**Highland Edge Walk** A81, 1½ miles/2½ km east of Aberfoyle (Braeval car park). 5 miles/8 km circular walk with high-level viewpoint.

**Wildering Forest Walks** Leanach car park, A821, 3½ miles/6 km north of Aberfoyle. Two walks (2 miles/3 km, 5 miles/8 km).

**Carron Valley** Spittal Bridge picnic place, off B818, 1 mile/1½ km west of Carron Bridge Hotel. Three walks (¾ mile/1 km, 1½ miles/2½ km, 3 miles/5 km).

**Strathyre** Forest Information Centre by A84 in Strathyre village. Leaflet showing hill walks, toilets, car park.

*Strathyre Forest Trail* From above car park (1½ miles/2½ km).

*Ben an t-Sithein walks* From above car park (4 miles/7 km) reaching to 1,750 feet/550 m, rocky in places, excellent views.

**Callander Crags** From main car park in Callander. 1¼ miles/2 km, steep in places.

**Kirkton Glen Walk** From behind Balquhidder Church (where Rob Roy is buried), minor road off A84. 3 miles/5 km.

# DUMFRIES AND GALLOWAY

## Antiquities

**Barsalloch Fort**  Off A747, 7½ miles/12 km west of Whithorn. AM; art; free. Remains of an Iron Age fort on a raised beach 60 feet/20 m above present shoreline.

**Birrens**  Off A74, 1 mile/1½ km north-east of Ecclefechan. Art; free. Extensively excavated remains of Roman fort; ditches and ramparts clearly visible.

**Burnswark**  2½ miles/4 km north-east of Ecclefechan. Art; free. Hill fort with extensive earthworks, possibly used by the Romans for training in siege warfare. May be associated with Birrens.

**Drumtrodden**  Off A714, 8 miles/13 km north-west of Whithorn. AM; art; free. Bronze Age cup and ring marks on a natural rock face. Nearby is a group of three standing stones.

**Kirkmadrine**  Off A716, 8 miles/13 km south of Stranraer. AM; art; free. The Kirkmadrine Stones, outside a small church, are among the earliest Christian monuments in Britain. They date from the 5th or 6th century AD.

**Laggancairn**  Kilgallioch (NX 222717). Nearest car access 9 miles/15 km north of Glenluce on Barrhill road, then 3 miles/5 km walk. AM; art; free. Two large standing stones with Dark Ages crosses.

**St Ninian's Cave**  From A747 south-west of Whithorn take minor road to Kidsdale, then ¾mile/1¼ km walk to coast. AM; art; free. The cave is said to have been the retreat of St Ninian, an early Christian saint. There are crosses carved on rocks.

**Torhouse**  Off B733, 3½ miles/6 km west of Wigtown. AM; art; free. Circle of 19 small standing stones, probably Bronze Age.

**Wren's Egg**  2 miles/3 km south-east of Port William, near Blairbuie farm. AM; art; free. Remains of an originally double stone circle.

# Castles

**Caerlaverock Castle**  Off B725, 9 miles/15 km south of Dumfries. AM; std. A 13th-century Maxwell stronghold, triangular in form, with very fine round towers. Interior reconstructed in 17th century as a Renaissance mansion. Caerlaverock NNR (NCC) with splendid birdlife is adjacent.

**Cardoness Castle**  A75, 1 mile/1½ km south-west of Gatehouse of Fleet. AM; std. A 15th-century tower house with four storeys and vaulted basement.

**Carsluith Castle**  A75, 7 miles/11 km west of Gatehouse of Fleet. AM; std; free. A 16th-century tower house on L-plan, now a roofless ruin.

**Castle of Park**  Off A75 at Glenluce, 9 miles/14 km east of Stranraer (art – exterior only; free). Castellated mansion built by Thomas Hay in 1590. May be opened to view in future.

**Craigcaffie Castle**  A77, 3½ miles/6 km north-east of Stranraer. Art; free. A 16th-century square tower on earlier foundations, said to have been laid on bags of wool.

**Drumlanrig Castle**  Off A76, 3 miles/5 km north of Thornhill. Open May-end Aug, Mon-Thur and Sat: 12.30-16.15; Sun: 14.00-17.15. Home of Duke of Buccleuch; 17th-century building in pink sandstone, fine furniture and paintings. Extensive grounds with nature trail, etc. also open.

**Hollows Tower**  A7, 5 miles/8 km south of Langholm. Art; free. A 16th-century stronghold, associated with reiver Johnny Armstrong.

**Lochmaben Castle**  A709, south shore of Castle Loch 9 miles/14 km east of Dumfries (art; free). Early 14th-century ruin, said to have been the birthplace of Robert Bruce.

**Orchardton Tower**  Off A711, 5 miles/8 km south-east of Castle Douglas. AM: std; free. (Key at nearby cottage.) Circular tower house unique in Scotland, dating from the mid-15th century.

**Threave Castle**  Off A75, 1½ miles/2½ km west of Castle Douglas. AM; std. 17th-century storeyed tower on an island, a Douglas stronghold from earlier times. Threave Gardens (NTS) and Wildfowl Refuge are nearby.

# Gardens

**Arbigland**  Off A710 by Kirkbean. 12 miles/19 km south of Dumfries. May-Sept, Tue, Thu and Sun: 14.00-18.00. Woodland, formal and water gardens overlooking a bay.

**Ardwell House**  Of A716, 10 miles/16 km south-east of Stranraer. Mar-Oct daily: 10.00-18.00. Spring flowers, shrubs, rock plants, walk round pond with views of Luce Bay. House not open.

**Castle Kennedy and Lochinch**  3 miles/5 km east of Stranraer on A75. Apr-Sept, daily: 10.00-17.00. Gardens on a peninsula between two lochs, world famous for rhododendrons, azaleas and magnolias. Lochside walks. Pinetum. Garden centre.

**Corsock House**  Off A712, 10 miles/16 km north of Castle Douglas. Open on Sundays in May only: 14.30-18.00, or by arrangement (tel. Corsock 250). Water gardens and rhododendrons. House not open.

**Galloway House**  ½ mile/1 km from Garlieston, 8 miles/13 km south of Wigtown. Open all year, daily. Walled garden shrubs, fine trees. House not open. Free (donations invited).

**Kinmount Gardens**  4 miles/7 km west of Annan. Easter-Nov daily: 10.00-17.00. Woodland walks, lakes, noted for azaleas and rhododendrons.

**Logan Botanic Garden**  Off B7065, 14 miles/22 km south of Stranraer. Apr-Sept daily: 10.00-17.00. Many plants from sub-tropical countries grow here. Also a fish pond, where fish can be fed by hand.

**Threave**  2 miles/3 km south of Castle Douglas on A75. Open all year, daily: 09.00-17.00. Rock and water gardens, daffodils in spring. Visitor centre open Apr-Oct. House not open. Threave Wildfowl Refuge (Nov-Mar only) is nearby (NTS).

# Historic Buildings and Monuments

**Bruce's Stone**  6 miles/10 km west of New Galloway by A712. Art; free. Granite boulder recording Bruce's victory in March 1307.

**Bruce's Stone**  East side of Loch Trool, 13 miles/20 km north of Newton Stewart. Art; free. Memorial stone on a viewpoint.

**Glenkiln**   Minor road 10 miles/16 km west of Dumfries. Art; free. Around a reservoir are set modern sculptures by Henry Moore, Epstein, Rodin and others.

**Gretna Smithies**   Off A74, 10 miles/16 km north of Carlisle. The famous smithies where runaway weddings were conducted. Open all year. Small museum of mementoes.

**Maxwelton House**   B729 near Moniaive, 13 miles/22 km north-west of Dumfries. May-Sept, Wed, Thur and some Suns: 14.00-17.00. 15th-century house, the birthplace of Annie Laurie. Display of early kitchen and dairy implements.

**Murray's Monument**   A712 7½ miles/12 km north-east of Newton Stewart. Art; free. Commemorates Dr Alexander Murray (1775-1813), a shepherd's son who became Professor of Oriental Languages at Edinburgh University.

**Rammerscales**   B7020, 2½ miles/4 km south of Lochmaben. Late Jun-mid-Sept, Tue, Wed, Thur and some Suns: 14.00-17.00. Georgian manor house dating from 1760. Collection of works by modern artists. Gardens and woodland walks.

# Industry

**Lighthouses**   Corsewall, tel. 077 685 220; Killantringan, tel. 077 681 202; Mull of Galloway, tel. 077 684 211.

**Logan Fish Pond**   Off B7065, 14 miles/23 km south of Stranraer. Easter-Sept Mon, Wed, Thur, Fri and Sun: 10.00-12.00; 14.00-17.30. Tidal pool in the rocks holding 30 fish tame enough to be fed by hand.

**North Glen Gallery**   Palnackie, 5 miles/8 km south-east of Castle Douglas. Open daily: 10.00-18.00. Glass-blowing, sculpture assembly, steel welding and cutting.

**Palgowan Open Farm**   Glen Trool. Open Easter and mid-May-end Oct, Sun-Fri. Book in advance (tel. Bargrennan (067 184) 231 or 227). Livestock, working dogs, making of shepherd's crooks, walking sticks, horncraft. *D.*

**Tongland Power Station**   A711, 2 miles/3 km north of Kirkcudbright. Jul-Sept, Mon-Sat: book tours in advance at Kirkcudbright tourist information centre or tel. 0557 30114. SSEB hydroelectric station and dam.

# Museums

**Craigcleuch Scottish Explorers' Museum**  B709, 2 miles/3 km northwest of Langholm. Easter and May-Sept daily: 10.00-17.00. Large house with exhibition of extraordinary tribal sculptures from Africa, Eskimo Canada, etc. Woodland walks in grounds.

**Galloway Deer Museum**  Clatteringshaws Loch, on A712, 6 miles/10 km west of New Galloway. Apr-Sept daily: 10.00-17.00. Tells the story of the red deer in Galloway, with other natural history items. Free.

**Gem and Rock Museum**  Chain Road, Creetown (A75). Open all year, daily: summer, 09.30-19.00; winter, 09.30-17.00. Large collection of gems, rocks and minerals from all over the world, plus displays of walking sticks and drinking mugs.

**Henry Duncan Museum**  At Ruthwell, 10 miles/16 km south-east of Dumfries, off B724. Open all year, daily. Memorial to the man who established the first Savings Bank in Scotland, in the cottage where he lived. Free.

**Museum of Scottish Lead Mining**  Goldscaur Road, Wanlockhead, on B797. Easter-Sept, daily: 11.00-16.00. Unique museum showing the history of lead mining in Scotland. There are 1½ miles/2 km of walkways, passing mine heads, pump engines, smelting sites, etc. Guided visits to a mine.

**Shambellie House**  ¼ mile/½ km north of New Abbey, 7 miles/12 km south of Dumfries, on A710. All year, Mon, Thur-Sat: 10.00-17.30; Sun: 12.00-17.30. Museum of costume; display changes annually. Free.

# Nature Reserves

**Caerlaverock** (NCC)  The reserve extends along six miles (10 km) of coastline between the estuaries of the River Nith and Lochar Water. The merse is one of the largest unreclaimed salt-marshes in Britain, and the most northerly breeding site of the natterjack toad. Winter roost for thousands of geese. Leaflets from NCC.

**Ken/Dee Marshes** (RSPB)  Escorted visiting by arrangement with warden: Drumglass, Laurieston, Castle Douglas DG7 2LZ.

**Mull of Galloway** (RSPB)  Access at all times to south cliffs near lighthouse. No warden.

# Religious Houses

**Chapel Finian**  Off A747, 12 miles/19 km west of Wigtown. AM; art; free. Small chapel or oratory dating from 11th century in an enclosure.

**Cruggleton Church**  B7063, 9 miles/15 km south of Wigtown. May-Sept daily, daylight hours (keys from farm). Free. Norman church with ruins of castle nearby.

**Dundrennan Abbey**  A711, 7 miles/11 km south-east of Kirkcudbright. AM; std. Cistercian house founded mid-12th century with much late Norman work.

**Glenluce Abbey**  A75, 2 miles/3 km north of Glenluce. AM; std. Vaulted chapter house. Cistercian, late 12th century.

**Lincluden College**  Off A76, 1 miles/1½ km north of Dumfries. AM: std. Closed Thur pm and all day Fri. 15th-century collegiate church and Provost's House with remarkable heraldic decorations.

**Queensberry Aisle**  Durisdeer, minor road off A702, 6 miles/10 km north of Thornhill. Art; free. Beautiful, small late 17th-century church, with splended monument to 2nd Duke of Queensberry and his Duchess.

**St Ninian's Chapel**  Isle of Whithorn, 3 miles/5 km south-east of Whithorn. AM; art; free. Ruins of a 13th-century chapel.

**Sweetheart Abbey**  A710, 7½ miles/12 km south of Dumfries. AM; std. Late 13th-century foundation by Devorgilla, widow of John Balliol (she also founded Balliol College in Oxford); now a romantic ruin.

# Visitor Centre

**Murray Forest Centre**  Off A75, ½ mile/1 km east of Gatehouse of Fleet. Apr-Sept daily: 09.00-18.00. Forestry exhibition and walks. Free.

# Walking

**Long-distance Path**  The Southern Upland Way starts at Portpatrick (near Stranraer) and crosses the region on its way to the Berwickshire coast. Information from the Countryside Commission for Scotland.

# Forest Walks

**Ae Forest**   Ae Village, minor road off A701 at Ae Bridge, 7½ miles/12 km north of Dumfries. Open all year. Two walks (1½ miles/2½ km or 2¼ miles/3½ km). *P.*

**Dalbeattie Forest**   A710, south of Dalbeattie town. Open all year. Craigmath Walk (1 mile/1½ km), Lochside Walk (2 miles/3 km) and Old Quarry Walk (3 miles/4½ km). *P.*

**Fleet Forest**   ½ mile/1 km east of Gatehouse of Fleet, on minor road signposted Cally Hotel. Open all year. Burn Walk (1 mile/1½ km), Mote Walk (to 12th-century Norman earthwork) (1½ miles/2½ km) and Coronation Walk (3 miles/4½ km).

## Galloway Forest Park

*Larg Hill and Bruntis Trails*   Palnure, A75, 3 miles/5 km south-east of Newton Stewart. Three walks (1¼ miles/2 km; 2½ miles/4 km and 4 miles/ 6 km). *P.*

*Loch Trool Forest Trail*   Caldons camp site; leave A714 9 miles/14 km north of Newton Stewart, following signs to Glen Trool (4½ miles/7 km). *P.*

*Stroan Bridge Trails*   ½ mile/1 km east of Glentrool village (3¾ miles/ 5½ km). *P.*

*Talnotry Trail*   A712, 7 miles/11 km north-east of Newton Stewart. Rugged walk of 4 miles/6 km. Wild goat park and Clatteringshaws Deer Museum nearby. *P.*

**Kilsture**   Hazlebank, A746 5 miles/8 km south of Wigtown (1 mile/ 1½ km). *P.*

**Mabie Forest**   Minor road off A710 5 miles/8 km south-west of Dumfries. Four walks (1 mile/1½ km, 2 miles/3 km, 3 miles/4½ km and 4 miles/6 km). *P.*

**Threave Countryside Trail**   Threave Garden, off A75, 2 miles/3 km west of Castle Douglas (¾ mile/1¼ km) (NTS). Visitor Centre open Mar-Oct. *P.*

# FIFE

## Antiquities

**Dogton Stone**   Off B922, 5 miles/8 km north-west of Kirkcaldy. AM; art; free. Ancient Celtic cross with traces of animal and figure sculpture. Enter by Dogton Farm.

## Castles

**Aberdour Castle**   A92, 10 miles/16 km east of Dunfermline. AM; std, not Mon am or Tues. Finely situated, overlooking the harbour, the oldest parts of the building date back to the 14th century. There is a splendid doocot nearby.

**Dunimarle Castle**   ¼ mile/½ km west of Culross, 4 miles/7 km east of Kincardine Bridge. Apr-Oct, Wed, Thur, Sat and Sun: 14.00-18.00. 19th-century building with notable paintings, small museum, gardens.

**Earlshall Castle**   Minor road 1 mile/1½ km east of Leuchars. Apr-Sept, Wed-Sun: 11.00-17.30. 16th-century fortified house with 5 foot/1.5 m walls, battlements and gun loops. Fine display of Scottish weaponry, gallery with painted ceiling. Garden also open.

**Kellie Castle**   Off A921, 10 miles/16 km south of St Andrews. NTS. Easter-end Sept, Sat-Thur: 14.00-18.00; Oct, Sat and Sun: 14.00-18.00. Started in 1336, mostly dates from 16th and 17th centuries, restored late 19th century by Lorimer. His grandson, the sculptor Hew Lorimer, lives there today. Extensive grounds and gardens open 10.00-dusk in season.

**Scotstarvit Tower**   Off A916, 3 miles/5 km south of Cupar. AM; std; free. Fortified tower from late 16th century. Hill of Tarvit (NTS, see also p. 101) is nearby.

## Country Parks

**Craigtoun**   On Claremont to Pitscottie road, 2 miles/3 km south-west of St Andrews (50 acres/20 ha). Former hospital grounds containing ponds (fishing), walks, bowling and putting greens, miniature railway, open-air theatre, ranger service. *D, P, T.*

**Lochore Meadows**  Access in Crosshill on B920 road (920 acres/327 ha). Mostly old colliery workings restored to woodland and Loch Ore itself. Sailing, fishing, walks, horse-riding, visitor centre, small nature reserve, ranger service. The head gear of the former Mary Pit is a feature.


# Gardens

**Dalgairn House**  In Cupar. Jun-Aug, Sat and Sun: 14.00-18.30. Unique collection of old-fashioned flowers, edible weeds and poisonous plants.

**Earlshall Castle**  Minor road 1 mile/1½ km east of Leuchars. Apr-Sept, Wed-Sun: 11.00-17.30.

**Kinross House**  B986, ½ mile/1 km south of Kinross. May-Sept daily: 14.00-19.00. Formal gardens overlooking Loch Leven (house not open).


# Historic Buildings and Monuments

**Michael Bruce's Cottage**  Kinnesswood, off A911, 4 miles/6 km east of Milnathort. Apr-Sept daily: 10.00-18.00 (key from Kinnesswood Garage). Birthplace of Michael Bruce, the 'Gentle Poet of Loch Leven', who died in 1767, aged 21.

**Culross**  Off A985, 4 miles/6 km east of Kincardine Bridge. Wonderfully preserved example of a small 16th/17th-century town (NTS). Notable buildings include the Palace, built by Sir George Bruce, which has remarkable painted ceilings; the Study, a tower house built in 1633; the Town House, built in 1526 and with a prison included; the Ark and the Nunnery. Palace AM; std opening. Study: Oct-Mar, Sat: 09.30-12.30 and 14.00-16.00; Sun: 14.00-16.00. Town House: Apr-Oct, Mon-Sat: 09.30-12.30 and 14.00-17.30; Sun: 14.00-17.30.

**Falkland Palace**  A912, 11 miles/18 km north of Kirkcaldy. NTS. Apr-Sept, Mon-Sat 10.00-18.00; Sun: 14.00-18.00; Oct, Sat: 10.00-18.00; Sun: 14.00-18.00. Renaissance-style palace of early 16th century, favoured seat of James V and Mary Queen of Scots. Royal (or 'Real') Tennis Court, gardens.

**Hill of Tarvit**  A916, 2 miles/3 km south of Cupar. Easter, then May-Sept, Sat-Thur: 14.00-18.00. Late 17th-century mansion remodelled by Lorimer in early 20th century; fine furniture, tapestries and paintings. Gardens open all year: 10.00-dusk.

# Industry

**North Carr Lightship** East Pier, Anstruther. Apr-Sept daily: 10.00-17.30. Once a working lightship, now a floating museum to show life on board such a vessel. Scottish Fisheries Museum nearby.

**Reediehill Deer Farm** Off B936, 3 miles/(5 km north of Auchtermuchty. Open all year, advance booking (tel. Auchtermuchty 369) essential. Management of deer explained, visitors can see feeding and may be able to handle deer. No dogs.

# Museums

**Crail Museum** 64 Marketgate, Crail (A917) Easter weekend and June-mid-Sept daily: 14.00-17.00. Tells the story of the town and surroundings.

**Fife Folk Museum** The Weigh House, Ceres, 3 miles/5 km south-east of Cupar on B940. Apr-Oct daily, except Tues: 14.00-17.00. Displays of life in Fife over the past century, including costumes and tools.

**Scottish Fisheries Museum** Harbourhead, Anstruther. Nov-Mar daily, except Tues: 14.00-17.00; Apr-Oct daily: 10.00-18.00 (Sun: 14.00-17.00 only). Closed Christmas and New Year holidays. Maritime museum including fishing vessels, equipment and an aquarium, housed in 16th- and 19th-century buildings.

**John McDouall Stuart Museum** Rectory Lane, Dysart, 2 miles/3 km north of Kirkcaldy, off A955. Museum to 19th-century explorer of Australia. June-Aug daily: 14.00-17.00. Free.

# Nature Reserve

**Tentsmuir Point** NNR (NCC) Between estuaries of rivers Tay and Eden. Access from A919 or B945. Large area of foreshore and dunes, trees and marsh. Many migrant birds. No visitor facilities.

# Private Railway

**Lochty Private Railway** B940, 7 miles/11 km west of Crail. June-early Sept, Sun only: 14.00-17.00. Steam train runs over 1½ miles/2½ km of track; passengers carried.

## Religious Houses

**Church of St Monan** St Monans, A917, 3 miles/5 km west of Anstruther. Art; free. 14th-century church built by David II with short square tower and fine groyned roof inside.

**Inchcolm Abbey** On Inchcolm Island in the Firth of Forth. Boat hire from Aberdour; check locally. AM; std. Well-preserved monastic buildings with 13th-century octagonal chapter house. Splendid views on the boat trip.

**Leuchars Norman Church** A919, 5 miles/8 km north-west of St Andrews. Art; free. One of the finest Norman churches in Scotland, with original chancel and apse.

**Lindores Abbey** Off A913, just east of Newburgh. Art; free. Ruins of a Benedictine foundation, dating from late 12th century.

## Forest Walks

**Edentown** B937, ½ mile/1 km west of Ladybank. Two walks (½ mile/1 km and 1 mile/1½ km). *D, P, T.*

**Craighall Den** ½ mile/1 km south of Ceres, on road to Lower Largo. Open all year. Nature trail walk of 1½ miles/2½ km along wooded glen with extensive bird and plant life. Guide from Ceres Post Office.

**Letham Glen** A915, Leven. Open all year. 1 mile/1¼ km nature trail through woodland. Pets corner, aviary, putting green. *P, T.*

**Ravenscraig Park** Near Kirkcaldy. Woodland trail of 2 miles/3 km. Open all year. *P, T.*

# GRAMPIAN

## Antiquities

**Brandsbutt**  On A96, 1 mile/1½ km north-west of Inverurie. AM; art; free (at Brandsbutt Farm). Pictish symbol stone with a well-preserved inscription in Ogham characters.

**Burghead Well**  At Burghead, 8 miles/13 km north-west of Elgin. AM; std; free. Rock-cut structure inside an Iron Age fort; possibly an early Christian baptistry.

**Cullerlie Stone Circle**  Off A974, 9 miles/15 km west of Aberdeen. AM; art; free. Circle of eight rough boulders.

**Culsh Earth House**  Near Tarland, on B9119, 13 miles/20 km north-east of Ballater (access by Culsh Farm). AM; std; free. Well-preserved Iron Age earth house.

**Dyce Symbol Stones**  At Dyce Old Church, 5 miles/8 km north-west of Aberdeen. AM; art; free. Two fine Pictish symbol stones.

**East Aquhorthies Stone Circle**  At NJ 733208, near Easter Aquhorthies Farm, 2½ miles/4 km west of Inverurie. AM; art; free. Small stone circle.

**Loanhead Stone Circle**  Off B9001, ¼mile/½ km north of Daviot. AM; art; free. Fine example of a recumbent stone circle.

**Maiden Stone**  At NJ 702247, off A96, 6 miles/10 km west of Inverurie. AM; art; free. Early Christian monument with a Celtic cross and Pictish symbols.

**Memsie Burial Cairn**  At NJ 977621, near Memsie village, 3 miles/5 km west of Fraserburgh. AM; art; free. Large stone cairn of *c.* 1500 BC.

**Peel Ring**  Off A980 at Lumphanan, 11 miles/18 km north-west of Banchory. AM; art; free. Early medieval earthwork, 120 feet/40 m in diameter, linked with Macbeth.

**Picardy Stone**  At NJ 610303, off A96, 8 miles/13 km south-west of Huntly. AM; art; free. Whinstone monolith with Celtic symbols.

**Sueno's Stone**  Beside B9011, 1 mile/1½ km north-east of Forres. AM; art; free. Remarkable monument, 20 feet/6 m high with elaborate carving.

**Tomnaverie Stone Circle**  At NJ 488035, 4 miles/7 km north-west of Aboyne. AM; art; free. Remains of a recumbent stone circle.


# Castles

**Auchindoun Castle**  Off A941 in Glen Fiddich, 3 miles/5 km south-east of Dufftown. AM; art; free. Massive ruin on hill top, surrounded by prehistoric earthworks. Viewed from outside only.

**Balmoral Castle**  A93, 8 miles/13 km west of Ballater. Grounds only, May-July daily (not Sun): 10.00-17.00. Not open when members of the Royal Family are in residence. Estate bought by Prince Albert in 1852, castle then rebuilt by William Smith of Aberdeen. The Queen and other members of the Royal Family normally spend 6-8 weeks here in the late summer.

**Balvenie Castle**  A941 Dufftown, 16 miles/25 km south of Elgin. AM; std. Ruins of a 14th-century moated Comyn stronghold.

**Braemar Castle**  A93 in Braemar. May-early Oct daily: 10.00-18.00. Son et Lumière sometimes in July-Aug. Castle rebuilt in 1748 after original building destroyed by fire. Central tower, underground prison. One of the centres of the 1715 Rising is nearby.

**Castle Fraser**  Off Craigearn to Dunecht road, 16 miles/25 km west of Aberdeen. NTS. Open May-Sept daily: 14.00-18.00. Spectacular building of late 16th/early 17th century, with large heraldic panel, exhibition telling the story of all the castles of Mar. Garden and grounds open all year.

**Cawdor Castle**  B9090 5 miles/8 km south-west of Nairn. May-early Oct daily: 10.00-17.00. Family home of the Earls of Cawdor for over 500 years, associated with Shakespeare's Macbeth. Notable gardens and woodland.

**Corgarff Castle**  Off A939, 15 miles/24 km north-west of Ballater. AM; std; 16th-century tower house converted into a garrison in mid-18th century.

**Craig Castle**  B9002, 12 miles/19 km south of Huntly. Summer months by arrangement, tel. Lumsden 202. 16th-century keep is 60 feet/20 m high, also fine courthouse.

**Craigievar Castle**  Off A980, 7 miles/11 km south of Alford. NTS. May-Sept, Sat-Thur: 14.00-18.00. Superbly preserved 17th-century tower and associated buildings with no later additions. Fine decorated ceilings. Grounds open all year.

**Craigston Castle**  Off B9105, 10 miles/16 km south-east of Banff. By arrangement, tel. King Edward 228. Early 17th-century seat of the Urquhart family, still in their ownership.

**Crathes Castle**  Off A93, 2½ miles/5 km east of Banchory. NTS. May-Sept, Mon-Sat: 11.00-18.00; Sun: 14.00-18.00. Outstanding example of a Scottish tower house dating from late 16th century, fine painted ceilings. Superb gardens (open all year, see p. 108), woodland walks.

**Delgatie Castle**  Off A947, 2 miles/3 km east of Turriff. By arrangement, tel. Turriff 3479. Tower house dating back to 12th century, home of the Hay family. Painted ceilings, portrait of Mary Queen of Scots, who stayed there in 1562.

**Drum Castle**  Off A93, 10 miles/16 km west of Aberdeen. NTS. May-Sept daily: 14.00-18.00. Late 14th-century granite tower adjoining 17th-century house, in the hands of the Irvine family for 600 years until 1975. Grounds (open all year) with rare trees and shrubs.

**Duffus Castle**  Off B9012, 4 miles/7 km north-west of Elgin. AM; std; free. Massive ruin of a motte and bailey castle with 14th-century tower.

**Dunnottar Castle**  A92, 1 mile/1½ km south of Stonehaven. Open all year, Mon-Sat: 09.00-18.00; Sun: 14.00-17.00 (closed Fri, Oct-Apr). Ruined fortress on 160 foot/50 m cliff where the Scottish regalia were hidden during the Wars of the Commonwealth.

**Eden Castle**  A947, 5½ miles/9 km south of Banff. Art; free. Ruin of a 17th-century home of the Nicholas family.

**Kildrummy Castle**  A97, 10 miles/16 km west of Alford. AM; std. Best example in Scotland of a 13th-century castle, with original round towers, hall and chapel, and later gatehouse. Dismantled in part in 1715.

**Muchalls Castle**  Off A92, 11 miles/18 km south of Aberdeen. May-Sept, Tue and Sun: 15.00-17.00 or by arrangement (tel. 0569 30217). Small 17th-century stronghold, overlooking the sea, with ornate ceilings and fine fireplaces.

*Craigievar Castle, south of Alford, Grampian*

**Pitcaple Castle**  A96, 4 miles/6 km north-west of Inverurie. Apr-Sept daily: 10.00-18.00. 15th-century Z-plan building, still used as a family home. Small museum.

**Slains Castle**  Off A975, 7 miles/11 km south of Peterhead. Art; free. Ruins of late 17th-century castle, built by the Earls of Errol. Said to have given Bram Stoker inspiration for the *Dracula* books.

**Tolquhon Castle**  B999, 7 miles/11 km east of Old Meldrum. AM; std. Early 15th-century rectangular tower, with later mansion. Carved panels, fine courtyard. See also *Pitmedden* under Gardens (p. 109).

# Country Parks

**Aden Estate**  Old Deer, A950/A92, 10 miles/16 km west of Peterhead (220 acres/89 ha). Woodland and parkland policies of Aden House. Campsite, walks, bridle paths, ranger. *P, T.*

**Balmedie**  On the coast, 8 miles/13 km north of Aberdeen (185 acres/ 75 ha). Good sandy beach, backed by dunes and links. Swimming, paths, wildlife. *D, P, T.*

**Haddo**  B9005, 7 miles/11 km north-west of Ellon (180 acres/73 ha). Grounds of Haddo House (NTS), woodland, parkland, lakes. Walks, information centre, ranger. *P, T.*

**Haughton House**  ½ mile/1 km north of Alford (75 acres/30 ha). Policies of Haughton House, woodland, banks of River Don. Nature trail, walks, riverside walk, play areas, ranger service. *P.*

# Gardens

**Anderson's Storybook Glen**  Maryculter, 5 miles/8 km west of Aberdeen. All year, daily: 09.00-20.00. Landscaped glen created by Anderson family with many attractions for children including Old Woman's Shoe and Teddy Bears' House.

**Arbuthnott House**  Off B967, 10 miles/16 km south-west of Stonehaven. By arrangement (tel. Inverbervie 226). Extensive formal garden. House also open (see p. 109).

**Crathes Castle**  A93, 2½ miles/5 km east of Banchory. Open all year, daily: 09.30-sunset. Yew hedges surround a series of small gardens Extensive woodland walks. See also Crathes Castle (NTS) (p. 106).

**Innes House**  B9103, 6 miles/10 km south-east of Elgin. May-Sept, Mon-Fri: 09.00-17.00. Herbaceous borders, roses, shrubs and interesting trees. Free (donations invited).

**Kildrummy Castle**  A97, 10 miles/16 km west of Alford. Apr-Oct, daily: 09.00-17.00. Interesting shrub and alpine garden. See also Castle (p. 106).

**Kincorth**  Off A96, 5 miles/8 km west of Forres. End May-end Sept, daily: 09.00-21.00. Borders, shrubberies and trees.

**Pitmedden**  Near Udny, B999, 14 miles/24 km north of Aberdeen. Open all year, daily: 09.30-sunset. Re-creation by NTS of 'Great Garden' laid out by Sir Alexander Seton in 17th century. Exhibition, museum of farm life. See also Tolquhon Castle (p. 108).

# Historic Buildings and Monuments

**Arbuthnott House**  Off B967, 10 miles/16 km south-west of Stonehaven. By arrangement (tel. 0561 226). Home of the Arbuthnott family since the 13th century. Present house is mainly 17th century. Garden also open to view.

**Balbithan House**  Off B977, 12 miles/20 km north-west of Aberdeen. By arrangement (tel. 0467 32282). Fine 17th-century house, with kitchen museum and exhibition of paintings; garden also open to view.

**Fasque**  B974, 2 miles/3 km north of Fettercairn. May-Sept, Sat-Thur: 13.30-17.30. 19th-century home of Mr Gladstone's father. Fine collection of estate papers and relics.

**Haddo House**  Off B999, 7 miles/11 km north-west of Ellon. May-Sept, daily: 14.00-18.00. NTS. Georgian (William Adam) mansion of 1730, home of the Earls of Aberdeen. Visitor centre and exhibition, programme of concerts and operas in small theatre. Grounds and Country Park open all year (see p. 108).

**Leith Hall**  B9002, 7 miles/11 km south of Huntly. May-Sept, daily: 14.00-18.00. NTS. Home of the Leith family for 300 years. Exhibition room includes a writing case presented by Bonnie Prince Charlie in 1746. Attractive grounds with paths, rock garden, wildlife hide are open all year.

**Nelson Tower**  Cluny Hill, Forres. Art; free. Viewpoint tower built in 1806 with fine views.

*Pitmedden Gardens, near Udny, Grampian*

# Industry

**Camphill Village** A93 at Bieldside, 5 miles/8km west of Aberdeen. Mon-Fri: 09.00-12.00; 14.00-17.00; Sat: 09.00-12.00. Free. Craft workshops where mentally handicapped adults make toys, woven goods, etc. Bakery and farm produce also sold.

**Fragrance of Scotland** (Ingasetter Ltd) North Deeside Road, Banchory. Open all year, Mon-Fri: 09.00-17.00. Manufacture of cosmetics explained and demonstrated. *D, P, T.*

**Glendronach Distillery** Forgue, near Huntly (A97). Open all year, Mon-Fri: tours at 10.00 and 14.00. Malting and whisky distilling. *P.*

**Glenfarclas Distillery** Off A95, 17 miles/26 km north-east of Grantown on Spey. Open all year, Mon-Fri: 10.00-16.30. Tour of distillery, exhibition and museum of old illicit distilling equipment. Free. *P.*

**Glenfiddich Distillery** North side of Dufftown. Open all year, Mon-Fri: 10.00-12.30 and 14.00-16.30. Full process from malting to bottling shown. *P.*

**Glengarioch Distillery** A947 at Old Meldrum. Sept-June by arrangement, tel. 06512 2706; at least 24 hours notice needed. Full distilling process shown, plus growing of tomatoes using waste heat. *P.*

**Glen Grant Distillery** A941 in Rothes. Easter-early Oct, Mon-Fri: 10.00-16.00. Full distilling process shown. *P.*

**Glen Livet Distillery** Ballindalloch, B9008, 10 miles/16 km north of Tomintoul. Easter-end Oct, Mon-Fri: 10.00-16.00. Full distilling process plus exhibition. *P.*

**Lighthouses** Girdle Ness, Aberdeen (tel. 0224 871142); Kinnairds Head, Fraserburgh (tel. 03462 2175); Inverbervie (tel. 05695 243); Covesea Skerries, Lossiemouth (tel. 034381 3064); Buchan Ness, Peterhead (tel. 0779 3488).

**Skene Lapidary Works** Garlogie School, Skene, on the A944, 10 miles/16 km west of Aberdeen. Open all year, Mon-Thur and Sat: 09.00-12.30 and 14.30-17.30. Free. Demonstrations of cutting and polishing of semi-precious stone.

# Museums

**Adamston Agricultural Museum**  2½ miles/4 km south of Huntly, off A96. Open all year, Wed, Sat and Sun: 09.00-17.00. Museum of rural and farm life situated on a working farm.

**Buckie Maritime Museum**  Clunie Place, Buckie. Open all year, except public holidays, Mon-Fri: 10.00-20.00; Sat: 09.30-12.30. Tells the history of fishing in the area since 1800. Free.

**Littlehaugh Agricultural Museum**  A941 at Rothes. All year, daily. Museum of former life on the farm.

**Pitmedden Garden**  Near Udny, B999, 15 miles/24 km north of Aberdeen. May-Sept, daily: 11.00-18.00. Exhibition of the history of gardening in Scotland (NTS; garden also open – see p. 109). Free.

**Tugnet Ice House**  Spey Bay, 3 miles/5 km west of Buckie. May-Sept, daily: 10.00-16.00. Free. Tells the story of the River Spey, its fishing and its wildlife, in a large former "ice house" dating from 1830.

# Nature Reserves

**Cairngorms** (NCC)  Largest NNR in Britain (over 100 sq. miles/25,000 ha). The area contains the largest area of high ground above 4,000 feet/1,200 m in Britain, arctic/alpine lochs and combinations of plateau, cliff and scree, with large tracts of native pinewood at lower levels. Access is unrestricted, but visitors are asked to co-operate with NCC and estates from August to late October, when deer culling takes place. Visitor centre and nature trail (leaflets) at Loch an Eilean, 3 miles/5 km south of Aviemore, and at Inverdruie, 1 mile/1½ km east of Aviemore on B970 (Rothiemurchus Estate). Part of the NNR is in Highland Region.

**Fowlsheugh** (RSPB)  Access at all times from small car park at Crawton, off A92, 3 miles/5 km south of Stonehaven. Wonderful seabird communities on spectacular cliffs. No warden.

**Loch of Strathbeg** (RSPB)  Near Fraserburgh. Visitors on Wed and Sun, all year: 10.00-17.00 by advance permit *only* from warden: The Lythe, Crimonmogate, Lonmay, Fraserburgh AB4 4UB. Leaflet.

**Longhaven Cliffs** (SWT)  Access from car park at Bullers of Buchan, on A92, 2 miles/3 km north of Cruden Bay. Magnificent cliff scenery, including the famous Bullers of Buchan, with varied and extensive seabird communities. No warden.

## Private Railway

**Alford Valley Railway** Murray Park, Alford. Narrow-gauge line in the park giving passenger rides. Apr, May and Sept, Sat and Sun: 11.00-17.00; July-Aug, daily: 11.00-17.00.

## Religious Houses

**Arbuthnott Church** Off B967, 10 miles/16 km south-west of Stonehaven. Art; free. Partly 13th-century church, with stained-glass windows depicting Faith, Hope and Charity.

**Ardclach Bell Tower** Off A939, 8 miles/13 km south-east of Nairn. AM; std; free. Two-storey 17th-century tower, used both for religious purposes and to warn people of danger.

**Birnie Church** Off A941, 3 miles/5 km south-east of Elgin. Believed to be the oldest parish church still in use in Scotland; it dates from early 12th century. Standing stones in churchyard.

**Crathie Church** A93, 8 miles/13 km west of Ballater. Apr-Oct, Mon-Sat: 09.00-18.00; Sun: 14.00-18.00. Free. Late 19th-century church, used for worship by members of the Royal Family while staying at Balmoral.

**Pluscarden Abbey** Off B9010, 6 miles/10 km south-west of Elgin. Open all year, daily: 05.00-20.30. Monastery founded in 1230, burned in 1390, restored by Benedictine monks in 1948. Free.

**St Mary's Church** Auchindoir, off A97, 11 miles/18 km south of Huntly. AM; art; free. Fine medieval parish church, now ruined.

## Visitor Centre

**Braeloine** Glen Tanar, near Aboyne (A93). Apr-Oct, daily: 10.00-17.00. Exhibition on the history of the estate and its wildlife. Walks and trails.

# Forest Walks

**Back o' Bennachie** Off B9002, 8 miles/13 km west of Inverurie. All year. Woodland and open hill, fine views. Three walks (½ mile/1 km, 1¼ miles/2 km and 5 miles/8 km). *P, T.*

**Kirkhill Forest** Between A93 and A944, 5 miles/8 km west of Aberdeen. All year. Woodland. Bloertops, Rotten of Gairn and Foggieton Brae each 1 mile/1½ km. Two Forest Lodge and Countesswells walks of 1 mile/1½ km and 1½ miles/2½ km. *P.*

**Laigh of Moray Forest** Monaughty, on Pluscarden road, 4½ miles/7 km west of Elgin. All year. Woodland. Four walks (1 mile/1½ km, 1¾ miles/ 3 km. 2½ miles/4 km and 5 miles/8 km). *P, T* (closed winter months).

**Mearns Forest** Drumtochty Glen, 5½ miles/9 km north of Laurencekirk. Apr-Oct. Woodland walk of 1 mile/1½ km. *D, P, T.*

**Mulloch (Banchory Forest)** 3 miles/5 km south-east of Banchory. One walk (½ mile/1 km). *P.*

**Shooting Greens (Banchory Forest)** On Feughside–Potarch road, 4 miles/7 km west of Banchory. All year. Three woodland walks (1 mile/1½ km, 2 miles/3 km and 3 miles/4½ km). *P, T.* (May-Sept).

**Speymouth Forest** A98, 1 mile/1½ km east of Fochabers. All year. 1½ miles/2½ km walk includes unique red 'earth pillars'. *P, T.*

**White Cow** On minor road, 2½ miles/4 km south of Strichen. Apr-Oct. Forest walk of 3 miles/4½ km includes badger sett and stone circle. *P, T.*

# Other Walks and Nature Trails

**Falls of Feakirk and Shenvault** The Beachans, 9 miles/16 km south of Forres, off A940. Trail follows the River Divie (1½ miles/2 km).

**Loch Dallas** The Beachans, as above. Path to Loch Dallas, passing the Ess Waterfall (1½ miles/2 km).

**Murray Park Nature Trail** Off A944, ¾ mile/1¼ km north of Alford. Woodland walk of 1¼ miles/2 km. Information and car park at Haughton House (see Country Parks p. 108). *P, T.*

# HIGHLAND

## Antiquities

**Achavanich**  East of Loch Rangag, off minor road, 6 miles/10 km north-west from Lybster. Art; free. A ritual site of standing stones in the form of an oval, open to the south. The higher stones still stand 5 feet above ground.

**Boarstone**  At Knocknagael, off B861, 2 miles/3 km south of Inverness. AM; art; free. Shaped slab 7 feet/2 m high, with an incised figure of a boar.

**Cairn of Get**  At ND 314410, 6½ miles/10 km south-west of Wick. AM; art; free.

**Clava Cairns**  Off B851, at NH 756445, opposite Culloden Battlefield. AM; art; free. Extensive Bronze Age grouping of cairns and standing stones.

**Cnoc Freiceadain**  At ND 012654, 3½ miles/6 km east of Reay. AM; art; free. Neolithic chambered cairn.

**Corrimony Cairn**  At NH 383303 in Glen Urquhart, 8 miles/14 km west of Drumnadrochit. AM; art; free. Neolithic chambered cairn with a circle of standing stones.

**Dun Dornadilla**  At NC 457450, south of Loch Hope (leave A836 20 miles/32 km north of Lairg). AM; art; free. A notable example of a broch.

**Glenelg Brochs**  In Gleann Beag, 2 miles/3 km south of Glenelg. AM; art; free. Dun Telve and Dun Troddan are fine examples of Iron Age brochs, with walls up to 30 feet/9 m high.

**Grey Cairns**  At Campster, 6 miles/10 km north of Lybster on Watten road. AM; art; free. Two megalithic chambered cairns.

**Hill o' Many Stanes**  At ND 295384, 3¼ miles/5½ km north-east of Lybster. AM; art; free. Neolithic site with almost 200 stones set out in 22 parallel rows.

# Castles

**Ardvreck Castle**  A837, 11 miles/19 km east of Lochinver on Loch Assynt. Art; free. Three-storeyed ruin of a 15th-century Macleod stronghold.

**Armadale Castle**  A851, ½ mile/1 km north of Armadale pier, Skye. Apr-Oct, Mon-Sat: 09.00-17.30, plus Sun: pm, June-Aug. 18th-century Macdonald castle, now a ruin, surrounded by fine woods and with the Clan Donald Centre attached. *D, P, R, T.*

**Castle Girnigoe**  On the road to Ness Head, 3 miles/5 km north of Wick. Art; free. A Sinclair stronghold on the cliffs alongside Castle Sinclair; both castles are now in a ruined state.

**Castle of Old Wick**  A9, 1½ miles/2½ km south of Wick. AM; art, except when adjacent rifle range in use; free. Ruin of 14th-century square tower on a headland.

**Castle Sinclair**  See *Castle Girnigoe.*

**Castle Tioram**  On an islet in Loch Moidart, 4 miles/7 km north of Acharacle. Art (when connecting sandbar enables access); free. A 14th-century Macdonald seat, accessible at low tide; it was burned in the 1715 Rising.

**Dunrobin Castle**  A9, 12½ miles/20 km north of Dornoch. Open mid-June-early Sept, Mon-Sat: 10.30-17.00; Sun: 13.00-17.00. Seat of the Earls and Dukes of Sutherland for centuries, superbly set in parkland overlooking the sea. Fine paintings and furniture.

**Dunsgiath Castle**  Tokavaig, 20 miles/32 km south of Broadford, Skye. Art; free. Another former Macdonald stronghold, with substantial remains.

**Dunvegan Castle**  A850, north-west coast of Skye. Easter-mid-Oct, Mon-Sat: 14.00-17.00 (June-Sept, from 10.30). Home of the chiefs of Clan MacLeod for 700 years. Many family treasures on display, including arms, books, paintings. Boat trips to seal colony. *P, R, T.*

**Eilean Donan Castle**  A87, 9 miles/14 km east of Kyle of Lochalsh. Easter-Sept, daily: 10.00-12.30 and 14.00-18.00. This is probably the castle most often featured on calendars of Scotland, picturesquely set in Loch Duich and connected to the mainland by causeway. Eilean Donan was restored comparatively recently after being in a ruined state since 1719. Incorporates a war memorial to the Clan Macrae.

**Knock Castle**  Off A851, 12 miles/19 km south of Broadford, Skye. Art; free. Another former Macdonald stronghold, in a ruined state.

**Urquhart Castle**  A82, 2 miles/3 km south of Drumnadrochit (west shore of Loch Ness). AM; std. Remains of a very large 14th-century castle in Grant hands from 1509, blown up in 1692 to prevent Jacobite occupation. A favourite place for 'monster-watching'!

# Gardens

**Castle of Mey**  A836, 7 miles/11 km west of John o' Groats. Occasional opening (see press). Spectacular situation looking out towards Orkney Islands. Home of HM the Queen Mother.

**Inverewe**  A832, 6 miles/10 km north-east of Gairloch. Open all year, daily: 09.00-21.00 or dusk. Magnificent subtropical garden started by Osgood Mackenzie in 1862. Palms, tree ferns, exotic plants from China. Visitor centre: Apr-Oct (NTS).

**Kyle House**  Kyleakin, Isle of Skye. May-Aug daily: 14.00-20.30. Rhododendrons, flowering shrubs. Fine views. Free (donations invited).

**Lochalsh Woodland Garden**  Off A87, 3 miles/5 km east of Kyle of Lochalsh. All year, daily. Wide variety of native and exotic trees and shrubs. Walks, indoor display (NTS).

**Nead an Eoin**  1¾ miles/3 km north of Plockton, 5 miles/8 km north of Kyle of Lochalsh. Mid-May-end Oct, Mon-Sat. Garden with woodland paths, superb views out to sea and northwards to Torridon. Free (donations invited).

# Historic Buildings and Monuments

**Bernera Barracks**  Glenelg, 9 miles/14 km west of A87 at Shiel Bridge. Art; free. Remains of large square barracks in use from 1722 until 1790, now in a ruinous state. Care needed.

**Commando Memorial**  A82 Spean Bridge, 11 miles/18 km north-east of Fort William. Monument by Scott Sutherland which commemorates the Commandos who used this area for training in the Second World War. Fine views.

**Fort George**   B9039, 8 miles/13 km west of Nairn. AM; std. Built in 1748 after the '45 Rising, the fort contains the regimental museum of the Queen's Own Highlanders.

**Glenfinnan Monument**   A830, 18 miles/30 km west of Fort William. Art; free (charge for exhibition). NTS. Commemorates the raising of the standard by Prince Charlie in 1745. NTS Visitor Centre and exhibition open Easter-Oct, 10.00-17.30 (09.30-19.00 in Jun-Aug). *D, P, R, T.*

**Indian Temple**   A9, Fynidh Hill above Evanton. Art; free. Said to be modelled on an Indian town gateway, it was erected by order of Sir Hector Munro in the late 18th century to ease local unemployment.

**Ruthven Barracks**   A9, ½ mile/1 km south of Kingussie. AM; art; free. Built after the 1715 Rising on a mound impressively sited. Blown up by retreating Highlanders after the Battle of Culloden in 1746.

**Well of the Seven Heads**   A82, west shore of Loch Oich. Art; free. Monument with inscription in Gaelic, Latin, French and English marking the execution of seven brothers for a clan murder.

## Industry

**Ardessie Fisheries**   A832, south side of Little Loch Broom. Easter-Oct, Mon-Sat: 10.00-19.00. Fish farm with brown and rainbow trout and salmon. Visitors can see the fish at all stages of growth and feed larger fish.

**Balnakiel Craft Village**   A838, 1 mile/1½ km west of Durness. Easter-Sept, daily: 09.30-18.00; free. Pottery, metalwork, weaving and other crafts demonstrated.

**Dounreay Atomic Energy Establishment**   10 miles/16 km north-west of Thurso. May-Sept, afternoons: 3 tours per day. Exhibition of nuclear energy and tour of reactors. *P, T.*

**Lighthouses**   Dunnet Head (tel. 084785 272); Cape Wrath (tel. 097181 230); Chanonry, Fortrose (tel. 0381 20478); Rubh Re, Gairloch (tel. 044585 220); Duncansby Head (tel. 095581 202); Ardnamurchan Point (tel. 09723 210); Tarbet Ness, Portmahomack (tel. 086287 210); Rosemarkie (tel. 03817 280); Strathy Point (tel. 06414 210); Holburn Head, Thurso (tel. 0847 2739); Noss Head, Wick (tel. 0955 2049).

**Tamdhu Distillery**   Knockando, B9102, 16 miles/25 km   north-east of Grantown on Spey. May-Sept, Mon-Fri: 10.00-16.00. See main distillery process from viewing gallery.

**Tomatin Distillery** A9, 15 miles/25 km south of Inverness. Mar-Oct, Mon-Fri at 15.00, only by prior arrangement (tel. 08082 234). See full process of whisky making. *D, P, T.*

# Museums

**Abriachan Croft Museum** The Schoolhouse, Abriachan, 10 miles/ 16 km south-west of Inverness, off A82. Apr-Oct, daily by arrangement (tel. 046-386 237). Museum of Highland life run by Inverness High School.

**Clan Donald Museum** Armadale Castle, Isle of Skye (½ mile/1 km from ferry pier, boats from Mallaig). Mid-Apr-mid-Oct, Mon-Sat: 09.00-17.30; also open June-early Sept, Sun: 14.00-17.30. Museum devoted to the history of Clan Donald.

**Clan Donnachaidh Museum** A9 at Calvin, 4 miles/7 km north of Blair Atholl. Apr-mid Oct, Mon-Sat: 10.00-17.30; Sun: 14.00-17.30. Free. Exhibits include items associated with the 1715 and 1745 Risings.

**Clan Macpherson Museum** Main Street, Newtonmore. May-Sept, Mon-Sat: 10.00-12.00 and 14.00-18.00. The story of Clan Macpherson and related families, including relics associated with Bonnie Prince Charlie. Free (donations invited).

**Curin Doll Museum** The Croft House, Curin, 12 miles/19 km from Muir of Ord, on the road to Strathconon. Mid-Apr-end Oct daily, except Tues: 14.00-18.00. Dolls of all ages and nationalities, dolls' houses, clothes and furniture.

**Gairloch Heritage Museum** In centre of village. Easter-Sept, Mon-Sat: 10.00-18.00. Folk museum depicting life in the area from earliest times to the present, with a furnished croft house.

**Highland Folk Museum** Duke Street, Kingussie. All year, except Christmas and New Year holidays: Mon-Fri: 10.00-15.00; also open Apr-Oct, Sat: 10.00-18.00 and Sun: 14.00-18.00. The first folk museum to be established in Scotland, in 1934, it includes a Lewis Black House and much agricultural equipment, waggons and carts.

**Hugh Miller's Cottage** Church Street, Cromarty. May-Sept, Mon-Sat: 10.00-12.00 and 13.00-17.00; also June-Sept, Sun 14.00-17.00. The home of the geologist and writer Hugh Miller with fine examples of his fossil collection (NTS).

**Lhaidhay Croft Museum**   1 mile/1½ km north of Dunbeath on A9. Apr-Sept, daily: 09.00-17.00. Furnished croft house with farm implements and machinery.

**Museum of Clan MacLennan**   Glenshiel, by Loch Duich, on A87. New museum telling the story of Clan MacLennan, with emphasis on piping and Highland dancing.

**The Piping Centre**   Boreraig, north-west of Dunvegan, Isle of Skye. Apr-Oct, daily: 10.00-18.00. The history of piping on display.

**Skye Black House Museum**   Colbost, by Dunvegan, Isle of Skye. Apr-Oct, daily: 10.00-19.00. Furnished as a 19th-century croft house with interesting folk material.

**Skye Cottage Museum**   Kilmuir, 2 miles/3 km south of Duntulm, Isle of Skye. Apr-Oct, Mon-Sat: 09.00-18.00. Furnished black house with farm and domestic implements, smithy and weaver's cottage.

**Skye Crofter's House Museum**   Luib, 7 miles/12 km north-west of Broadford, Isle of Skye. Apr-Oct, daily: 10.00-18.00. Black house showing living conditions 80 years ago.

**Strathnaver Museum**   Bettyhill, 30 miles/48 km west of Thurso on A836. June-Sept, Mon-Sat: 14.00-17.00. Museum of the 'clearances', including posters painted by local children.


# Nature Reserves

**Beinn Eighe** (NCC) A superb mountain reserve located near Kinlochewe, it was the first NNR to be declared in Britain and in October 1983 was awarded the Diploma of the Council of Europe, the first site in Scotland to receive this award. Visitor centre off A832, 3 miles/5 km north-west of Kinlochewe (summer months only). Mountain trail, nature trail, leaflets, warden.

**Cairngorms**   See under Grampian Region (p. 112).

**Corrieshalloch Gorge** (NCC/NTS) On A835, 1 mile/1½ km west of junction with A832. A magnificent example of a box canyon formed by the cutting back of the Abhainn Droma through hard, horizontally disposed rock. The walls are up to 200 feet (60 m) high and the Falls of Measach tumble into the gorge at its deepest point. Walks with suspension bridge across the gorge.

*Balmoral Castle and Deeside, Grampian*

**Craigellachie** (NCC)  Situated immediately west of Aviemore, the reserve contains fine birchwoods and open moorland rising to 1,700 feet (510 m). Footpath access from Aviemore.

**Culbin Sands** (RSPB)  Access at all times along shore from Kingsteps, 1 mile/1½ km east of Nairn, on minor road past golf course. No warden.

**Handa** (RSPB)  This beautiful island contains very varied plant and bird life. Day visits (not Sundays), April-August, by boat from Tarbet. 3 miles/5 km nature trail, leaflet, information point. RSPB members can stay in bothy – apply to Edinburgh Office (address on p. 173).

**Insh Marshes** (RSPB)  Parking and information point on B970, 2 miles/3½ km east of Kingussie. Open Apr-July, Wed, Fri and Sun: 10.00-17.00; Aug, Wed only: 10.00-17.00. Winter visiting by arrangement with warden: Ivy Cottage, Insh, Kingussie PH21 1NT.

**Inverpolly** (NCC)  Large, remote area on west coast between Ullapool and Lochinver. Information centre (summer months) at Knockan, on A835, 15 miles/24 km north of Ullapool. Knockan Cliff Nature Trail shows classic geological area with a section of the Moine Thrust zone. Great diversity of habitats. Leaflets available.

**Loch Fleet** (SWT)  Large sandy tidal basin north of Dornoch, can be viewed from the A9 or minor road to Skelbo. Important feeding area for wintering ducks; large number of waders. No warden.

**Loch Garten** (RSPB)  Off B970, between Boat of Garten and Nethy Bridge. Famous for its ospreys. Nest can be viewed from observation post daily mid-Apr-late Aug, 10.00-20.00. Access within bird sanctuary strictly confined to marked path. Warden; leaflets.

# Private Railway

**Strathspey Railway**  Stations at Aviemore (link with BR) and Boat of Garten. Mid-May-mid-Oct, Sat and Sun: 12.00-18.00, plus July-Aug, Mon, Tue and Wed: 09.30-18.00. Timetables available locally. Part of the former Highland Railway, restored by volunteers and now with a steam train operating. Small museum with railway relics.

# Religious Houses

**Beauly Priory**   A9 at Beauly, 12 miles/19 km west of Inverness. AM; std. Ruins of a 13th-century Valliscaulian foundation.

**Croick Church**   Minor road to Strath Carron, 10 miles/16 km west of Ardgay. Church built by Thomas Telford which has inscriptions on the windows left by crofters during the 19th-century clearances.

**Fort Augustus Abbey**   A82, Fort Augustus. Apr-Oct, daily: guided tours at 10.30, 11.40, 15.30 and 16.15. Benedictine Abbey occupying site of a former fort. Monks from here set up the first experiment in hydro power in the 1890s.

**St Mary's Chapel**   Crosskirk, off A836, 6 miles/10 km west of Thurso. Art; free. Roughly constructed chapel, probably 12th century, in Irish style.

# Visitor Centres

**Cairngorm Pine Forest Centre**   On ski road 3 miles/5 km east of Aviemore. All year daily: 10.00-18.00 or dusk if earlier. Forest interpretation centre showing the flora and fauna of the surrounding area.

**Clan Donald Centre**   A851 Armadale, Isle of Skye (½ mile/1 km from pier – regular ferry from Mallaig). Apr-Oct, 09.00-17.30. Museum of the Isles Exhibition, woodland gardens, arboretum, guided walks, children's play area, restaurant, audio-visual programme.

**Culloden**   B9006, 5 miles/8 km east of Inverness, Easter-end May and Sept-mid Oct, daily: 10.00-18.00; June-Aug, daily: 09.30-20.00. Exhibition of the Battle of Culloden in 1746, audio-visual programme, memorials (NTS).

**Darnaway Estate Visitor Centre**   Off A96, 3 miles/5 km west of Forres. Easter and mid May-mid Sept, daily: 11.00-17.30. Exhibition of the Moray Estates, nature trails, woodland walks, farm exhibits. Forest walks with Ranger, Wed and Sun, tours of estate Tues and Sun: 14.15.

**Farigaig Forest Centre**   B862, 17 miles/30 km south of Inverness. Easter-Oct: 09.30-19.00. Shows the development of forestry in the Great Glen. Free.

**Glencoe**   A82, 2 miles/3 km east of Ballachulish. Easter-mid-May and mid-Sept-mid-Oct, daily: 10.00-17.00; mid-May-mid-Sept, daily:

10.00-19.00. General information on the area and the Massacre of Glencoe, 1692. Walks and trails (NTS). Ranger service.

**Glenfinnan**  A830, 18 miles/30 km west of Fort William. Easter-end May and Sept-mid-Oct, daily: 09.30-18.00. June-Aug, daily: 09.30-20.00. Commemorates the 'raising of the standard' in 1745 and shows how the Rising developed (NTS).

**Landmark Visitor Centre**  Carrbridge, A9, 8 miles/13 km north of Aviemore. All year. Triple-screen audio-visual show of Highland history, plus excellent exhibition. Craft and bookshop, restaurant, walks and trails.

**Loch an Eilean**  B970, 2½ miles/4 km south of Aviemore. May-Sept, daily. Traces the history of the Scots pine forest of Rothiemurchus from earliest times to the present. Free. (NCC).

**Rothiemurchus Visitor Centre**  Cairngorm road, 2 miles/3 km north of Aviemore. Open all year. Information on the estate, guided walks with ranger, etc. 'Whisky centre' nearby.

**Torridon**  A896, 8 miles/13 km west of Kinlochewe. June-Sept, Mon-Sat: 10.00-18.00; Sun: 13.00-18.00. Small centre with deer museum amd audio-visual show. Ranger service and guided walks programme (NTS).

# Wildlife Parks

**Highland Wildlife Park**  B9152, 7 miles/11 km south of Aviemore. Mar-Oct: 10.00-18.00. Drive-through section with red deer, bison, Highland cattle, etc. Also on display are wolves, wildcats, eagles and many other species, all in a beautiful natural setting. Exhibition, children's section. *D, P, R, T.*

# Walking

**Long-distance Walks**  The West Highland Way enters the region near Bridge of Orchy and runs from there to its northern terminus in Glen Nevis via Victoria Bridge, Glencoe, Kinlochleven and the Lairig Mor.

The Speyside Way runs from near Aviemore to the Moray Firth at Speymouth, but the southern half is currently still under negotiation.

Details of both paths from the Countryside Commission for Scotland.

# Forest Walks

**Borgie**  Off A836 at Borgie Bridge, 5 miles/8 km east of Tongue. Short walk along the coast in mature woodland (½ mile/1 km). *P.*

**Craig Phadraig**  Leachkin road off A9, 2 miles/3 km west of Inverness. Walk of 1 mile/1½ km to a hilltop with fine views. *P, G.*

**Culloden Forest**  Culloden, 5 miles/8 km east of Inverness. Marked trail of 2 miles/3 km with indicators showing different types of trees, wildlife, etc. *P, G.* NTS Visitor Centre at Culloden Battlefield nearby (see p. 123 above).

**Dog Falls**  Glen Affric road, west of A831 at Cannich; *P* in 2 miles/3 km. Pinewoods, loch and open hill (2½ miles/4 km). *P.*

**Farigaig**  B852, 17 miles/30 km south of Inverness (east side of Loch Ness). Forest trail of 1 mile/1½ km. *P, G.*

**Glen Garry**  A87, 2 miles/3 km west of Invergarry. Woodland and fine waterfall (1½ miles/2½ km or 2¼ miles/3½ km). *P.*

**Glen More**  East end of Loch Morlich, 6 miles/10 km east of Aviemore on Cairngorm road. Three trails, each about 1½ miles/2½ km. *P, G.*

**Glen Righ**  Off A82 (Inchree), 8 miles/13 km south of Fort William. Corrychurrachan walk, forest tracks (¾ mile/1¼ km). Waterfall walk to 120 feet/40 m falls (1 mile/1½ km). *P.*

**Glenvarragill**  A850, ½ mile/1 km south of Portree, Skye. Woodland walk with good views to Raasay (2¼ miles/3½ km). *P.*

**Inchnacardoch**  Off A82, 2 miles/3 km north-west of Fort Augustus. Woodland trail of 1 mile/1½ km. *P, G.*

**Kyle of Sutherland**  Off A837, between Rosehall and Invershin. Four walks (1-2¼ miles/1½-3½ km). *P, G.*

## Lochaber Forest

*Achriabhach*, in Glen Nevis, 5 miles/8 km south of Fort William. Forest walk of 1 mile/1½ km. *P, G.*

*Clunes*, B8005, 12 miles/20 km north-east of Fort William. Three walks (1½ miles/2½ km; 2 miles/3 km; 5½ miles/9 km). *P, G.*

*Glen Loy*, off B8004, 7 miles/11 km north of Fort William. Two walks (½ mile/1 km; 2 miles/3 km). *P, G.*

*Lairigmor*, from Blar a'Chaoruinn minor road, 4 miles/7 km south of Fort William (1 mile/1½ km). *P, G.*

**Morangie**  A9, 4 miles/7 km west of Tain. Steep hillside path with good views (1 mile/1½ km). *P.*

**Reelig Glen**  Off A9, 8 miles/13 km west of Inverness. Forest walk of 1 mile/1½ km. *P, G.*

**Rock Wood Ponds**  B970, Glen Feshie, 8 miles/13 km south of Aviemore. Walk of 1 mile/1½ km circling attractive small lochs, with information boards. *P.*

**Rogie**  A832, 1 mile/1½ km north-west of Contin. System of walks in woodland to Rogie Falls and beyond, if desired (up to 2 miles/3 km). *P, T, I.*

**Rumster**  Off A9, ½ mile/1 km south of Lybster, 2 miles/3 km along road to Achavanich. Woodland walk of 1½ miles/2½ km. *P.*

**Slattadale**  A832, 7 miles/11 km south-east of Gairloch, on Loch Maree. Forest trail of ½ mile/1 km, and path on open ground of 5 miles/8 km. *G.*

**Storr**  A855, 7 miles/11 km north of Portree, Isle of Skye. Steep walks with superb views and fantastic rock scenery around. Two walks, each of 2 miles/3 km. *P.*

**Strome Wood**  A890 junction with old Strome Ferry road. Woodland walk with fine views over Loch Carron (1 mile/1½ km). *P.*

**Torrachilty**  Off A834, 7½ miles/12 km west of Dingwall. Woodland trail with viewpoints (3¼ miles/5 km). *P, G.*


# Nature Trails

**Beinn Eighe**  A832, 2 miles/3 km north-west of Kinlochewe. Short trail and mountain trail. Information from Beinn Eighe NNR visitor centre (see Nature Reserves, p. 120).

**Craigellachie**  From Aviemore Centre (A9). Trail of 1 mile/1½ km through nature reserve. *P.*

**Knockan Cliff**   A835, 13 miles/21 km north of Ullapool. May-Sept only. Trail showing geological features (1½ miles/2½ km). Information from visitor centre. *P, T, G.*

**Strontian Glen**   1½ miles/2½ km north of Strontian (off A861). Woodland and moorland (4 miles/6 km or 7 miles/11 km). *P, G.*

# Other Walks

**Black Isle**   The book *Walks in the Black Isle*, available from tourist information centres at Muir of Ord and North Kessock, lists 18 short walks in the Black Isle area, mostly under 3 miles/5 km.

**Lochalsh**   Series of walks on NTS Balmacara estate. Information from visitor centre in grounds of Lochalsh House, south of A87, 3½ miles/5½ km east of Kyle of Lochalsh. Ranger. *P, T.*

# LOTHIAN

## Antiquities

**Cairnpapple Hill**  Off B792, 3 miles/5 km north of Bathgate. AM; std (Apr-Sept only); charge. Neolithic sanctuary and Bronze Age cairn, excavated and laid out.

**Castle Law**  At Glencorse, off A702, 7 miles/12 km south of Edinburgh. AM; art; free (key from Crosshouse Farm, Milton Bridge). Small Iron Age hill fort and earth house.

**Chesters**  At NT 507782, 1 mile/1½ km south of Drem. AM; art; free. Fine example of an Iron Age fort with ramparts.

**Doon Hill**  At NT 685757, near Dunbar, off A1. AM; art; free. Anglo-Saxon site.

## Castles

**Blackness Castle**  B903, 4 miles/7 km north-east of Linlithgow. AM; std. Oct-Mar closed Mon pm and Tues. A 15th-century stronghold, one of the four castles which, under the Articles of Union, had to be left fortified. Has since served as a gunpowder store and a youth hostel!

**Borthwick Castle**  A7, 13 miles/21 km south of Edinburgh. Art; free (seen from outside only). 15th-century tower house with twin towers and two wings.

**Crichton Castle**  B6367, 7 miles/11 km south-east of Dalkeith. AM. Apr-Sept, Mon-Sat: 09.30-19.00; Sun: 14.00-19.00; Oct-Mar, Sat: 09.30-16.00; Sun: 14.00-16.00. Elaborate castle with 14th-century keep and decorated stonework, once held by the Earls of Bothwell.

**Dirleton Castle**  A198, 7 miles/11 km west of North Berwick. AM; std. Ruins dating back to mid-13th century of castle, first put under siege by Edward I in 1298. Garden with 17th-century bowling green and fine yew trees.

*Dirleton Castle, East Lothian*

**Hailes Castle** Off A1, 5 miles/8 km east of Haddington. AM; std. Castle dates from 13th to 15th century with fine 16th-century chapel. Mary Queen of Scots stopped here after leaving Borthwick Castle in 1567.

**Ochiltree Castle** 3 miles/5 km south-east of Linlithgow. Easter-Sept, Sun: 14.00-18.00 plus July-Sept, Wed: 14.00-18.00 and Bank Holiday Mondays: 14.00-18.00. 16th-century castle with collections of arms and armour, paintings and period furniture.

**Tantallon Castle** A198, 3 miles/5 km east of North Berwick. AM; std. (Oct-Mar closed Tue). 14th-century Douglas stronghold, dramatically sited on a cliff top. The castle was attacked and badly damaged by General Monck's forces in 1651.

# Country Parks

**Almondell and Calder Wood** Off A71, at east end of East Calder village. 10 miles/16 km west of Edinburgh (220 acres/90 ha). Linear park following the valley of the River Almond, the two sections being linked by a footpath. Nature trail, ranger service, walks, camping area. *P, T.*

**Beecraigs Wood** Off minor road, 2 miles/3 km south of Linlithgow (800 acres/321 ha). Largely wooded area with plenty of footpaths. Fishing on a reservoir, deer farm, ranger service, trout farm, visitor centre.

**Hillend** A702, 5 miles/8 km south of Edinburgh (96 acres/39 ha). Area on the northern slope of the Pentland Hills featuring a large dry-ski slope used both for training and for competitive events. Visitor centre, café, walks, chairlift, rangers. *P, R, T.*

**John Muir Park** A1087 on west edge of Dunbar and A198 ½ mile/1 km north of Tyninghame (1,670 acres/675 ha). Takes in 8 miles/13 km of coastline, with good sandy beaches and the Tyne estuary. Considerable nature conservation interest. Ranger service. Golf course, caravan site at Dunbar end. *P, T.*

**Vogrie** A68, 10 miles/16 km south of Edinburgh (257 acres/104 ha). Policies of Victorian country house with fine areas of woodland. Extensive path network. Field studies, ranger service. (Access from B6372 between Ford and Gorebridge.)

# Gardens

**Hopetoun Gardens**   Off A904, 1 mile/1½ km west of South Queensferry. Open all year daily: 10.00-17.30. Walled garden, formal rose garden, woodland garden. Donations. See also *Hopetoun House* below.

**Inveresk Lodge**   South side of Musselburgh, off A6124. Open all year, Mon, Wed and Fri: 10.00-16.30. Shrubs, climbing roses, walks (NTS). Lodge not open.

**Tyninghame**   1 mile/1½ km north of A1, between Dunbar and East Linton. June-Sept, Mon-Fri: 10.30-16.30. Walled garden, woodland walks, apple garden, borders. Ruins of St Baldred's Church.

# Historic Buildings and Monuments

**Hopetoun House**   Off A904, 1 mile/1½ km west of South Queensferry. May-Sept, daily: 11.00-17.00. 18th-century country house, home of the Marquess of Linlithgow. Notable portraits and fine furniture. Extensive grounds with deer, rare breeds of sheep, rose garden, visitor centre, stables museum. *D, P, R, T.*

**House of the Binns**   Off A904, 4 miles/7 km east of Linlithgow. NTS. May-Sept, Sat-Thur: 14.00-17.30. Early 17th-century house with fine ceilings. Closely associated with the Dalyell family; the present tenant is Labour MP Tam Dalyell. Grounds (open 10.00-19.00) have fine views across the Firth of Forth.

**Kinneil House**   Off A904, 4 miles/7 km north-west of Linlithgow. AM; std, closed Tues pm and all Fri. 16th-century seat of the Dukes of Hamilton, with splendid paintings and decorated ceilings. In an outhouse here, James Watt worked on his earliest steam engines.

**Lennoxlove House**   B6369, 1 mile/1½ km south of Haddington. Apr-Sept, Wed, Sat and Sun: 14.00-17.00. 17th-century mansion named after a Duchess of Lennox, 'La Belle' Stewart.

**Winton House**   B6355, 6 miles/10 km south-west of Haddington. By arrangement, tel. 0875 340222. Superb Renaissance house dating from 1620, with carved stone chimneys, decorated ceilings, paintings and fine furniture. Conducted tours only.

# Industry

**Preston Mill**  Off A1, at East Linton, 6 miles/10 km west of Dunbar. NTS. Apr-Oct, Mon-Sat: 10.00-12.30, 14.00-17.30; Sun: 14.00-17.30; Nov-Mar, Sat: 10.00-12.30, 14.00-16.30; Sun: 14.00-16.30. Water-mill beautifully restored to full working condition. Nearby is Phantassie Doocot.

# Museums

**Dunbar Lifeboat House**  The Harbour, Dunbar, off A1. May-Sept, Mon-Sat: 14.00-17.00. Working lifeboat house with display of models of boats and equipment used by lifeboatmen. Free.

**Museum of Flight**  East Fortune Airfield, 4½ miles/7 km south of North Berwick. July and Aug daily: 10.00-16.00 and on 'open days' (see press). Aircraft, engines and rockets, includes a Second World War Spitfire. Free.

**Myreton Motor Museum**  Aberlady. May-Oct, daily: 10.00-18.00; Nov-Apr, daily: 10.00-17.00. Large display of cars, cycles, motor-cycles, accessories and motoring paraphernalia.

**Prestongrange Mining Museum**  Morrison's Haven, 7½ miles/11 km east of Edinburgh, on B1348. Open all year, except public holidays, daily: 08.30-16.00 (Sat by arrangement). Working engines and mining artefacts. Volunteers at work on Sundays. Free (donations invited).

# Nature Trails

**Barns Ness**  3 miles/5 km south-east of Dunbar. Walk of 2½ miles/4 km. Open all year. Guide book from Mr Lough, Catcraig Cottage, Barns Ness. *P.*

**Hopetoun House**  Off A904, 1 mile/1½ km west of South Queensferry. May-Sept. Walk of 2 miles/3 km through woods and parkland with deer, St Kilda sheep, etc. *P, R, T.* Seasonal ranger service. See also Historic Buildings, p. 131.

**Yellowcraigs**  Off B1345, 3 miles/5 km west of North Berwick. Open all year. Woodland walk. Guide book and details from Senior Ranger, Craigielaw Cottages, Longniddry (087 57 265).

# Religious Houses

**Abercorn Church** Off minor road (signposted Hopetoun House), 2 miles/3 km from A904 at South Queensferry. Art; free. Medieval church with a fine 'laird's loft' and several unusual gravestones.

**Dunglass Collegiate Church** West of A1 (signposted Bilsdean, 1 mile/1½ km north of Cockburnspath). AM; art; free. Church founded mid 15th century, with nave, choir, transepts and tower still standing.

**Rosslyn Chapel** Off A703, 7½ miles/12 km south of Edinburgh. Apr-Oct, Mon-Sat: 10.00-13.00 and 14.00-17.00. 15th-century chapel with superb sculpture and the richly-decorated Prentice Pillar.

**Torphichen Church and Preceptory** B792, 5 miles/8 km south of Linlithgow. Church: art; free. Preceptory: AM; std. In the 15th century the Preceptory was the Scottish centre for the Knights Hospitaller of St John, and contains an exhibition on the Knights. The church is 16th century on the site of an older building, and has seats marked for Knights of the Order of St John.

**White Kirk** A198, 5 miles/8 km south-east of North Berwick. Art; free. 15th-century church with wooden spire. A large 16th-century barn nearby was once used to store grain for the monks of Holyrood Abbey in Edinburgh.

# Walking

**Pencaitland Railway Walk** Saltoun Station, B6093, 3 miles/5 km east of Dalkeith. Disused railway line giving walk of 5 miles/8 km. Open all year. Guide book from Council Buildings in Haddington.

**Pressmennan Forest Trail** B6370 Stenton, 6 miles/10 km south-west of Dunbar. Walk of 2 miles/3 km by Pressmennan Lake through woodland with fine views. *P.*

# STRATHCLYDE

## Antiquities

**Auchagallon**  At NR 893347, 4 miles/7 km north of Blackwaterfoot, Isle of Arran. AM; art; free. Stone circle.

**Bar Hill**  Excavated fort and section of ditch on Antonine Wall, above village of Twechar, 2 miles/3 km east of Kirkintilloch. AM; art; free. Access on foot only.

**Cairn Ban**  3½ miles/6 km north-east of Kilmory village, off A841, Isle of Arran. AM; art; free. A notable Neolithic long cairn. There are many other cairns in the area.

**Dunadd Fort**  At NR 837936, off A816, 4 miles/7 km north-west of Lochgilphead. AM; art; free. The site of the ancient capital of the kingdom of Dalriada in the 5th-9th centuries AD.

**Kilberry**  Kilberry Castle is off B8024, 20 miles/32 km south-west of Lochgilphead. At NR 710643 is a fine group of sculptured stones. AM; art; free.

**Kildalton**  7½ miles/11 km north-east of Port Ellen, Islay. AM; art; free. In the churchyard are two fine Celtic crosses and sculptured slabs.

**Kilmartin**  A816, 7½ miles/12 km north of Lochgilphead. The area contains many interesting monuments and relics. In Kilmartin churchyard are fragments of two crosses. At Baluachraig (NR 832971), Ballygowan (NR 820974), Cairnban (NR 838910) and Kilmichael Glassary (NR 858935) are cup-and-ring marked rocks. There are cairns at Dunchraigaig (NR 833968) and Nether Largie (NR 832985), and a stone circle at Temple Wood (NR 826979). All art; free.

**Torr a' Chaisteil**  At NR 922233, Corriechravie, Isle of Arran. AM; art; free. Iron Age hill fort.

**Torrylin**  At NR 955211, ½ mile/1 km south-west of Kilmory, Isle of Arran. AM; art; free. Neolithic chambered cairn.

# Castles

**Ardrossan Castle**  Overlooking Ardrossan Bay. Art; free. Ruin of 12th-century castle destroyed by Cromwell's troops. Fine views across to Arran.

**Bothwell Castle**  A74, Uddingston, 7 miles/11 km south-east of Glasgow. AM; std, closed Weds pm and all Thur. 15th-century Douglas stronghold, set above the Clyde Valley.

**Brodick Castle**  1 mile/1½ km north of Brodick, Isle of Arran. Apr-Sept, daily: 13.00-17.00. NTS. Ancestral seat of the Dukes of Hamilton, oldest parts date from 13th century with 17th- and 19th-century additions. Fine furniture, paintings, silver and porcelain. Ground (open all year) now a Country Park (see p. 136).

**Carleton Castle**  A77, 6 miles/10 km south of Girvan. Art; free. Ruined watchtower, one of several along this coast.

**Carnasserie Castle**  Off A816, 9 miles/15 km north of Lochgilphead. AM; art; free. Ruin of the house of John Carswell, first Protestant Bishop of the Isles. His translation of Knox's *Liturgy* was the first book to be printed in Gaelic (1567).

**Carrick Castle**  West side of Loch Goil, 5 miles/8 km south of Lochgoilhead. Art; free. Rectangular castle from early 16th century, used as a prison and burned by Atholl forces in 1685.

**Castle Sween**  Minor road on east side of Loch Sween, 15 miles/23 km south-west of Lochgilphead. AM; art; free. Possibly the oldest stone castle on the Scottish mainland, dating from mid-12th century and largely destroyed in 1647.

**Craignethan Castle**  Off A72 at Crossford, 5 miles/8 km north-west of Lanark. AM; std. Extensive remains of Hamilton stronghold including ornately-designed tower house.

**Culzean Castle**  A719, 12 miles/20 km south of Ayr. Apr-Sept, daily: 10.00-18.00; Oct, daily: 12.00-17.00. NTS. Adam building of 1770s including fine ceilings and superb oval staircase. Display of General Eisenhower mementoes; he stayed here several times. Grounds are a Country Park (see p. 137).

**Duart Castle**  Off A849 on east shore of Mull. May-Sept, daily: 10.30-18.00. MacLean stronghold since 1390. Castle was restored from a ruined state in 1911 by Sir Fitzroy MacLean, former Chief Scout. Display of Scouting material. *P, R, T.*

**Dunstaffnage Castle** Off A85, 4 miles/6 km north of Oban. AM; std; closed Thur pm and all day Fri. Well-preserved example of a 13th-century castle with round towers, set overlooking the mouth of Loch Etive. *P.*

**Eglinton Castle** Off A78, 2 miles/3 km north of Irvine. Art; free. Late 18th-century castle with central tower 100 feet/30 m high.

**Inverary Castle** ½ mile/1 km north of Inverary. Apr-June and Sept-mid Oct, Mon-Sat (not Fri): 10.00-12.30, 14.00-17.30; Sun: 14.00-17.30. July-Aug, Mon-Sat: 10.00-17.30; Sun: 14.00-17.30. Seat of the Dukes of Argyll for 250 years. Magnificent interior decoration, paintings by Gainsborough, Raeburn, etc. Badly damaged by fire in 1975, but superbly well restored.

**Kilchurn Castle** Off A85, 2 miles/3 km west of Dalmally. AM; art; free (exterior view only). 15th-century Campbell keep with late 17th-century additions. Interior not open.

**Loch Doon Castle** On Loch Doon road, 5 miles/8 km south of Dalmellington (A713). AM; art; free. Early 14th-century castle moved from its original site, which was drowned by a hydro scheme.

**Lochranza Castle** Off A841 on north coast of Isle of Arran. AM; std; free. 14th-century castle with two square towers, where Robert the Bruce is said to have landed at the start of his fight for Scottish independence.

**Rothesay Castle** A886, Rothesay, Isle of Bute. AM; std, closed Thur and Fri am. Founded in 12th century, the castle was stormed by Norse invaders in 1230. The circular courtyard is unique in Scotland.

**Torosay Castle** A849, 1½ miles/2½ km south of Craignure, Mull. May-Oct, Mon-Fri (also Sun in July-Aug): 10.00-18.00. Victorian castle with fine rooms. Grounds (open all year) include terraced gardens. Narrow-gauge railway runs to Craignure.

## Country Parks

**Balloch Castle** South end of Loch Lomond, ½ mile/1km north of Balloch (200 acres/81 ha). A mixture of woodland and parkland, with a length of loch shore and the start of the River Leven. Footpaths, slipway, nature trail, ranger. Balloch Castle itself is the Nature Conservancy Council regional office. *P, T.*

**Brodick Castle** 1 mile/1½ km north of Brodick, Isle of Arran (178 acres/72 ha). Extensive area of gardens and woodland surrounding Brodick Castle (NTS, see p. 135). The footpath to Goat Fell, Arran's most popular mountain, starts from the park, Children's play area, footpath network, wheelchair trail, nature trail, ranger service, visitor centre (summer months). *D, P, R, T.*

**Calder Glen** South-east of East Kilbride, access from A726 East Kilbride – Strathaven road (373 acres/151 ha). The park follows the River Calder with an area of open land at its southern end, including a golf course. Visitor centre, small zoo, nature trail, ranger service, play areas. *P, R, T.*

**Castle Semple** Off A760, on east side of Lochwinnoch (445 acres/180 ha). Park centres on Castle Semple loch and is mainly devoted to water-based recreation. Footpaths link the loch area to Parkhill Wood. There is an RSPB reserve with visitor centre and hides within the park. *P, R, T.*

**Culzean Country Park** Off A719, 12 miles/20 km south-west of Ayr (575 acres/233 ha). A very varied area, including rocky coast with small bays, woodland, a disused railway line (now a footpath) and Culzean Castle itself. Castle and park are both administered by the National Trust for Scotland. Visitor centre, camping/caravan site, guided walks (ranger), cliff walk. *D, P, R, T.*

**Dean Castle** Off B7038, on north-east edge of Kilmarnock (200 acres/81 ha). Woods, parkland, two streams. Visitor centre in the Dower House (ranger), castle keep with museum of medieval musical instruments and armour, nature trail, play areas. *D, P, R, T.*

**Gleniffer Braes** On southern outskirts of Paisley (access from Gleniffer Road) (1,186 acres/480 ha). Extensive area of hill ground sloping down towards the town. Much of the area is used for agriculture. Footpaths, ranger service, nature trail, pony-trekking, orienteering, fishing. *P, T.*

**Muirshiel** Off B786, 3 miles/5 km north-west of Lochwinnoch (80 acres/32 ha). The former policies of Muirshiel Estates, mainly rough woodland and moorland. Nature trail, footpaths, ranger, visitor centre. *P, T.*

**Palacerigg** 2 miles/3 km south-east of Cumbernauld, on Greengairs road (632 acres/256 ha). Former farmland, now used for mainly informal recreation; it includes a number of 'wildlife pens'. Countryside centre, ranger, bridleways, sailing, fishing, golf course. *P, R, T.*

**Pollok** Off A77 or B768, in the south-west part of Glasgow (360 acres/146 ha). Mature woods and parkland with extensive footpath system, formal gardens, restored mill. Ranger service. Pollok House itself is open 10.00-16.00 and the park also contains the Burrell Collection of art treasures. *P, T.*

**Strathclyde** Astride the M74 motorway; access from A725 or A723, between Motherwell and Hamilton (1,600 acres/648 ha). Created from derelict land, the eastern part contains Strathclyde Loch, much used for sailing, rowing and fishing. Other recreation includes horse-riding, and there are playing fields with woodland walks. The western part includes the Raith Haugh nature reserve and the Hamilton Mausoleum. Visitor centre, rangers, water sports, caravan and camp site, nature trails. *P, R, T.*

# Gardens

**Achamore House** Isle of Gigha. All year, daily: 10.00-dusk. Rhododendrons, camellias, semi-tropical plants. Tel. 05835 217 for ferry information.

**Achnacloich** Loch Etive-side, 3 miles/5 km east of Connel. Apr-mid-June, Mon-Fri: 08.00-22.00. Flowering shrubs, azaleas, rhododendrons, primulas.

**An Cala** B844, ¼ mile/½ km from Easdale, Argyll. Apr-Sept, Mon and Thur: 14.00-18.00. Water and rock gardens, cherries, azaleas, roses.

**Ardanaiseig** Loch Awe-side, off B845, 22 miles/35 km east of Oban. Apr-Oct, daily: 10.00-dusk. Rhododendrons, rare shrubs and trees; superb views.

**Ardchattan House** North side of Loch Etive, 7 miles/11 km north-east of Oban. Apr-Sept, daily: 08.00-19.00. Borders, shrubs, wild garden, roses. Garden planned for maximum effect July-Sept. Ardchattan Priory nearby was the seat of the last Gaelic Parliament (not normally open).

**Arduaine** A816, 20 miles/32 km south of Oban on Loch Melfort. Apr-Oct, Sat-Wed: 10.00-18.00. Coastal garden noted for rhododendrons and azaleas. Water garden and rock garden.

**Bargany** B734, 4 miles/7 km south of Girvan. Feb-Oct: 10.00-19.00 (16.00 in winter). Woodland garden, rock garden, rhododendrons; fine autumn colours.

**Barguillean** In Glen Lonan, 3 miles/5 km south of Taynuilt. Apr-Oct, daily: 09.00-dusk. Garden round loch with shrubs, flowering trees, rhododendrons, daffodils in spring.

**Brodick** Isle of Arran. Open all year, daily: 10.00-17.00. Woodland garden, exceptional rhododendrons, subtropical plants, formal garden. See also Brodick Castle (p. 135) and country park (p. 136).

**Carradale House Gardens** B842, 12 miles/19 km north of Campbeltown. Apr-Sept, daily: 10.00-16.00. Walled garden, wild garden with paths and iris pond.

**Crarae Woodland Garden** A83, 10 miles/16 km south-west of Inverary. Mar-Oct: 08.00-18.00. Rhododendrons, exotic trees and shrubs. Fine colours in spring and autumn. Plant sales.

**Glenapp Castle Gardens** A77, 15 miles/24 km south of Girvan. Mid-Apr-end Sept, Sun-Fri: 10.00-17.00. Extensive gardens with terraces, woodland walks and walled garden.

**House of Treshnish** Isle of Mull, B8073, 14 miles/22 km west of Tobermory. Apr-Oct, daily: 08.00-21.00 or dusk. Woodland garden, flowering shrubs, spectacular sea views.

**Kilmun Arboretum** A880, 5 miles/8 km north of Dunoon. Open all year, daily. Fine collection of specimen trees on hillside above Holy Loch. Free.

**Kiloran Gardens** Isle of Colonsay. Open all year, daily. Noted for rhododendrons and shrubs, including magnolias.

**Strone, Cairndow** A83/A815, 12 miles/20 km east of Inveraray. Apr-Oct, daily: 09.00-21.00 or dusk. Daffodils, rhododendrons, exotic shrubs, pinetum containing one of Britain's tallest trees.

**Torosay Castle** Isle of Mull, A849, 1½ miles/2½ km south of Craignure. May-mid Oct, Mon-Fri, also Sun in July-Aug: 10.00-18.00. Extensive gardens with statue walk designed by Sir Robert Lorimer. Narrow gauge railway. See also Torosay Castle (p. 136).

**Younger Botanic Garden** A815, 7 miles/11 km north of Dunoon. Apr-Oct, daily: 10.00-18.00. Extensive woodland gardens with superb avenue of sequoia trees.

# Historic Buildings and Monuments

**Bell Obelisk** Off A82, west of Bowling. Art; free. Memorial, at Douglas Point, to Henry Bell, who build the *Comet*, the first passenger steamship to operate on the Clyde.

**Blantyre Obelisk**   Off B815, 2 miles/3 km west of Erskine. Art; free. Tall monument to the 11th Lord Blantyre, who died in the Brussels riots in 1830.

**Cameron Loch Lomond**   A82, 2 miles/3 km north-west of Balloch (west shore of Loch Lomond). Apr-Oct, daily: 10.00-17.00. Cameron House has displays including an Oriental room, a collection of over 1,000 different whisky bottles, and model aircraft. The extensive grounds include a wildlife park, gardens, facilities for water sport, etc.

**Finlaystone**   Off A8, just west of Langbank. Open all year, Mon-Sat: 09.00-17.00; Sun: 14.00-17.00. House includes fine furniture and a large international collection of dolls. Extensive grounds include a garden centre, formal gardens, woodland walks, jogging trail, summer ranger service. *P, R, T.*

**Macintyre Monument**   Off A85, 2 miles/3 km south of Dalmally, on a minor road. Art; free. Monument to the Gaelic poet Duncan Ban Macintyre (1724-1812).

*In Covenanting Footsteps*, published by the Clyde Valley Tourist Board, gives details of many Covenanter sites in the area.

## Industry

**Auchentoshan Distillery**   Off A82 at Duntocher, 10 miles/16 km west of Glasgow. Open by arrangement (24 hours notice required); tel. 0389 78561. Tour of distillery, reception area and shop. *P, R, T.*

**Ben Cruachan Power Station**   A85, 6 miles/10 km west of Dalmally. Easter-Oct, daily: 09.00-17.00. Visitor Centre, visit to turbine room inside the mountain by minibus. Also steep footpath to dam and reservoir with fine views. *P, R, T.*

**Bowmore Distillery**   Bowmore, Islay. Mar-Oct, Mon-Fri and Oct-Mar, Tues and Thur: 10.30 and 14.30. Tour obligatory. All aspects of distilling. Prior notice to 049 681 441 requested. *P, T.*

**Hunterston Nuclear Power Station**   Off A78, 4 miles/7 km south of Largs. May-Sept, daily: book in advance (tel. 0294 823668). Tour of power station with viewing galleries, displays, audio-visual presentation. *P, T.*

**Laphroaig Distillery**   Port Ellen, Islay. Jan-May and Sept-Dec: 11.00 and 15.00 by prior arrangement (tel. 0496 2418 or 2393). Malting, manufacture and warehousing of malt whisky. *P, R, T.*

**Lighthouses**  Mull of Kintyre (tel. 058683 234); Turnberry, Girvan (tel. 06553 225).

**Port Askaig Distillery**  Bunnahabhain, 6 miles/10 km north of Port Askaig, Islay. Open all year, Mon-Fri: 10.00-16.00 (prior notice on Port Askaig 646 preferred). Distillation of malt whisky. *P, R, T.*

**Scottish White Heather Farm**  Toward, 5 miles/8 km west of Dunoon. All year, Mon-Sat: 09.00-18.00; Sundays by arrangement (tel. 036987 237). Visitors can see the extensive heather gardens overlooking the Firth of Clyde. *P, R, T.*

**Tobermory Distillery**  Main Street, Isle of Mull. Open all year, Tue and Thur: 14.00. Distillation of malt whisky. *P, T.*

# Museums

**Appin Wildlife Museum**  Appin Home Farm, A828, 20 miles/32 km north of Oban. All year, daily: 10.00-18.00. Small display of wildlife material collected by the owner. Free (donations invited).

**Arran Heritage Museum**  Rosaburn, Brodick. Mid-May-mid-Sept, Mon-Fri: 10.30-13.00, 14.00-16.30. A collection of traditional buildings, including smithy, 19th-century cottage, stable block, milling parlour.

**Auchindrain Museum of Country Life**  5½ miles/9 km south of Inveraray, on A83. Apr-May, Sept: 11.00-16.00 (closed Sat); June, July, Aug, daily: 10.00-17.00. Original farming township furnished in 19th-century style, with displays showing agricultural changes at the time. Demonstrations.

**Auchinleck Boswell Mausoleum and Museum**  Church Hill, Auchinleck, on A76. By arrangement, tel. 0290 20757. Memorial and museum to James Boswell, the biographer of Dr Johnson, and William Murdoch, pioneer of gas lighting.

**Bute Museum**  Stuart Street, Rothesay, Oct-Mar, Tue-Sat: 14.30-16.30; Apr-Sept, Mon-Sat: 10.30-12.30, 14.30-16.30. Exhibits of local natural and social history, with good archaeological specimens.

**Cnoc Breac Folk Museum**  Mingarry, 17 miles/27 km south of Lochailort on A861. Mid-May-end Sept, Mon-Fri: 10.30-13.00, 14.00-17.30; Sat: 10.30-14.00. Museum of local history and culture, run by community co-operative.

**Easdale Island Folk Museum**  Easdale Island, off Seil Island (Oban-Campbeltown road, A816). Apr-Oct, Mon-Sat: 10.30-17.30; Sun: 10.30-17.00. History of life on the island and the slate industry, which operated from the mid-18th century until 1911.

**Glencoe and North Lorn Folk Museum**  In Glencoe village. May-Sept, Mon-Sat: 10.00-17.30. Restored cottage with displays of domestic and agricultural interest including Jacobite relics. Special display relating to the slate industry in Ballachulish.

**Iona Abbey Museum**  Isle of Iona (ferry from Fionnphort on Mull). Mar-Oct, daily: 10.00-17.00. Small museum displaying relics from the abbey. Free.

**Museum of Islay Life**  Port Charlotte, Isle of Islay. Apr-Sept, Mon-Fri: 10.00-17.00, and Sun: 14.00-17.00; Oct-Mar, Mon-Fri: 10.00-16.30. Outstanding exhibits include carved stones from 6th century and prehistoric food vessels, plus display of social, domestic and agricultural life.

**Museum of the Cumbraes**  Garrison House, Millport, Isle of Cumbrae. June-Sept, Tue-Sat: 10.00-16.30. Natural history, domestic and industrial items from the island's past. Free.

**Old Byre Heritage Centre**  Dervaig, Isle of Mull. Apr-Oct, daily: 10.30-17.30. Tells the story of a Mull crofter's life at the time of the Clearances, and the changes that took place afterwards.

**Weaver's Cottage**  Kilbarchan, 2 miles/3 km west of Johnstone, via A737. May, Sept and Oct, Tue, Thur, Sat and Sun: 14.00-17.00; June-Aug, daily: 14.00-17.00. 18th-century weaver's cottage with handlooms and other weaving equipment (NTS).

# Nature Reserves

**Ardmore** (SWT)  Car park access from A814, Cardross-Helensburgh road. Views over extensive mudflats and foreshore of Clyde estuary with waders and wildfowl. Nature trail. No warden.

**Falls of Clyde** (SWT)  New Lanark. Spectacular valley woodland along River Clyde. Nature trail, visitor centre. Ranger: 4 Caithness Row, New Lanark.

**Loch Lomond** (NCC) Reserve is at south-east corner of loch and consists of five islands: Inchcailloch, Torrinch, Creinch, Clairinsh and Aber Isle, with part of the shore and lower reaches of River Endrick. Directly on the Highland Boundary Fault. Leaflets on the nature trail on Inchcailloch (boats from Balmaha). Parties should contact the warden in advance at The Castle, Loch Lomond Park.

**Lochwinnoch** (RSPB) Visitor centre off A760, ½ mile/1 km east of Lochwinnoch (towards Paisley). Part of the Clyde-Muirshiel Regional Park, the reserve has a wide variety of birdlife which can be viewed from the tower at the visitor centre and from two hides. Open all year, Thur-Sun: 10.00-17.15.

## Religious Houses

**Ardchattan Priory** On the north side of Loch Etive, 3 miles/5 km north-east of Connel. AM; art; free. Remains of a Valliscaulian house founded in 1230, the scene of a Parliament convened by Robert the Bruce in 1308, it was burned by Cromwell's troops in 1654. Ardchattan House gardens are nearby.

**Bowmore Round Church** Bowmore, Islay. Art; free. Circular church of French design, built in 1769.

**Crossraguel Abbey** A77, 2 miles/3 km south-west of Maybole. AM; std, but closed Thur pm and Fri. Remains of a Cluniac monastery founded in mid-13th century and inhabited by Benedictine monks until late 16th century.

**Iona** Access by ferry (no cars) from Fionnphort, at west end of Mull, on A849 (also boat trips from Oban in summer). Holy site where St Columba founded a monastery in 563. The restored abbey is the home of the Iona Community. Many Scottish kings and chiefs are buried on Iona, and there are many remains of religious buildings, crosses, etc.

**Saddell Abbey** B842, 9 miles/15 km north of Campbeltown. Art; free. Ruin of 12th-century abbey founded by Somerled, Lord of the Isles.

## Visitor Centres

**Arran Nature Centre** Northern outskirts of Brodick, Isle of Arran. Open all year, daily: 10.00-18.00. Natural history of the island; book and craft shop.

**Culzean Castle and Country Park**  A719, 12 miles/20 km south of Ayr. Apr-Sept, daily: 10.00-18.00; Oct, daily: 12.00-17.00. Information centre, talks and films, walks with rangers, aviary and orangery.

**Kelburn Country Centre**  A78, 2 miles/3 km south of Largs. Easter-Sept, daily: 10.00-18.00. Exhibitions, nature trails, pony-trekking, children's adventure course based on 'square' of farm buildings.

**Land o' Burns Centre**  Alloway, 2 miles/3 km south of Ayr. Open all year: 10.00-17.00 (21.00 in summer). Agricultural museum exhibition, audio-visual programme on life of Robert Burns. Free; charge for audio-visual show.

**Strathyre Forest Centre**  Strathyre village, A84, 10 miles/16 km north of Callander. May-Sept: 09.00-19.00. Display of forestry and recreation within forests. Free.

## Wildlife Interest

**Cameron Loch Lomond**  A82, 2 miles/3 km north-east of Balloch, west shore of Loch Lomond. Easter-Oct, daily: 10.00-17.00. Wildlife park with bears and other animals, and large leisure area including loch frontage. See also under Historic Buildings (p. 140).

**Sea Life Centre**  A828 11 miles/18 km north of Oban. Apr-Oct, daily: 10.00-17.00 (20.00 June-Aug). Marine life in all its forms, from small fish to octopus and seals. 'Touch tank' for children. *D, P, R, T.*

**University Marine Biological Station**  Great Cumbrae Island – ferry from Largs. Open all year, Mon-Fri: 09.30-12.30, 14.00-17.00; Apr-Sept, Sat: 09.30-12.30; June-Sept, Sat: 14.00-17.00. Marine biological research station, at Keppel Pier near Millport. Work of the station is displayed and there are aquaria.

## Walking

**Long-distance Paths**  The southern end of the West Highland Way, from Glasgow to Fort William, is in Strathclyde Region, as far as Strathblane. The path officially starts in Milngavie.

**Isle of Bute**  Information from the Museum, Stuart Street, Rothesay on walks at the following locations: Bull Loch, Etterick Bay, Kingarth, Loch Fad, south end of Bute.

# Forest Walks

**Ardentinny to Carrick** Off A880, ½ mile/1 km north-west of Ardentinny village. Woodland and lochside walk; 5 miles/8 km, or 10 miles/16 km, if returning by same route. Rugged terrain. *P, T.*

**Ardgartan** A83, 3 miles/5 km west of Arrochar.

*Loch Goil walk* Forest and open moor, rising to 1,250 ft/400 m. Rugged walk of 5 miles/8 km one way. May be closed during deer stalking season. *P, G.*

*Coilessan Glen* Alternative route to Loch Goil (6 miles/9½ km). Notes as above. *P, G.*

*Corran Lochan* Strenuous 12 miles/19 km walk with fine views, end at Loch Goil or return to Ardgartan by same route. Notes as above. *P, G.*

**Ardgartan (Lettermay)** Minor road 1½ miles/2½ km south of Lochgoilhead. Two walks: to Strachur (6 miles/9½ km) and to Loch Eck (also 6 miles/9½ km). Both walks cross rugged open terrain with fine views. *P, G.*

**Ardmore** Minor road to Glengorm, 5 miles/8 km north-west of Tobermory, Mull. Walk circles the northern point of Mull with very fine views (4 miles/6½ km). *P.*

**Aros Park** A848, 1½ miles/2½ km south of Tobermory, Mull. Footpath around wooded lochan (¾ mile/1½ km); also cliff walk back to Tobermory. *P, T.*

**Balmaha** B837 at Balmaha, 5 miles/8 km north of Drymen. Two walks: steep walk of 1½ miles/2½ km with views of Loch Lomond; gentle walk of 1¾ miles/3 km through forest. *P, T, G.*

## Barcaldine Forest

*Beinn Lora* A828, 2 miles/3 km north of Connel Bridge. Forest and open hill with good views (1 mile/1½ km or 3 miles/4½ km).

*Eas na Circe* A828, 10 miles/16 km north of Connel Bridge. Walk of 2½ miles/4 km, steep in parts. *P.*

*Glen Dubh* Sutherlands Grove, A828, 7 miles/11 km north of Connel Bridge. Mixed woodland and river gorge (¾ mile/1¼ km or 1½ miles/3 km). *P, G.*

**Carradale Forest** B842, 10 miles/16 km north of Campbeltown, Kintyre. Shore walk through forest with fine views to Arran (6½ miles/

L

10 km). Sally's Walk through ornamental trees and shrubs (1 mile/1½). Visitor centre in summer months. *P, T, G.*

**Fearnoch**   B845, 3 miles/5 km south of Taynuilt. Trail partly through old broadleaved forest with remains of charcoal burning sites (2½ miles/4 km). *P.*

**Glendaruel**   A8003, 5 miles/8 km north of Tighnabruaich. Woodland and shore walk of 1½ miles/2½ km. *P, G.*

**Inverliever**   Minor road on west side of Loch Awe, 10 miles/16 km south of Taynuilt. Mature woodland (2¼ miles/3½ km). *P, G.*

**Knapdale Forest**
*Loch Coille Bhar*   Off B8025, 2 miles/3 km south of Crinan Canal. Woodland and loch, very scenic (1 mile/1½ km or 3 miles/4½ km). *P, G, I.*
*Oib Mhor*   Location as above. Archaeological walk with points of interest marked (6 miles/9½ km). *P, G, I.*

**Puck's Glen**   By A815, 6 miles/10 km north of Dunoon. Woodland walks, steep in parts. Several walks (1½-4 miles/2½-6½ km). *P.*

**Sallochy Trail**   Minor road, 3 miles/5 km north of Balmaha, east shore of Loch Lomond. Forest trail of 1¼ miles/2 km (West Highland Way passes through this area). *P, G.*


# Nature Trails

**Balloch**   Starts at gate of Loch Lomond Park at north end of Balloch village. Woodland and loch shore (1½ miles/2½ km). See also Balloch Castle (p. 136).

**Corehouse**   Off A72 at Kirkfieldbank, 2 miles/3 km south of Lanark. Woodland and gorge of River Clyde (1½ miles/2½ km or 3 miles/4½ km). Permit needed for some parts – apply Mrs Beal, 18 Ladyacre Road, Lanark (tel. 0555 3829).

**Cornalees Bridge**   Minor road 2 miles/3 km east of A78 at Inverkip. Wooded glen and moorland (1½ miles/2½ km). *P, I.*

**Lunga**   A816, 22 miles/35 km south of Oban. Woodland, hill and farmland with captive birds and animals in wildlife reserve (1 mile/1½ km) (new trails being added). Apr-Sept only. *P, G, R, T.*

# TAYSIDE

## Antiquities

**Aberlemno**  On B9134, 5 miles/8 km north-east of Forfar. AM; art; free. Four sculptured stones, one in the churchyard with Pictish symbols.

**Ardestie and Carlungie**  B962, 6 miles/10 km east of Dundee. AM; art; free. Two examples of large earth-houses. Ardestie is 80 feet/24 m long and Carlungie, which is 1 mile/1½ km north, is larger at 150 feet/45 m.

**Ardoch Roman Camp**  A822 at Braco, 10 miles/16 km south of Crieff. Art; free. Large Roman station of 2nd century AD.

**The Caterthuns**  At NO 555668 and 548660, 5 miles/8 km north-west of Brechin. AM; art; free. Two Iron Age hill forts, Brown and White Caterthun, with ramparts and ditches.

**Eassie**  Off Glamis-Meigle road, 7 miles/11 km south-west of Forfar. AM; art; free. A fine early Christian sculptured stone, in Eassie kirkyard.

**Fowlis Wester**  Off A85, 5 miles/8 km north-east of Crieff. AM; art; free. Pictish stone of 8th century with clear carvings, opposite St Bean's Church (13th century).

**St Orland's Stone**  At NO 401500, near Cossans Farm, 3½ miles/6 km west of Forfar. AM; art; free. Sculptured slab.

**Tealing Earth-House**  Off A929, 5 miles/8 km north of Dundee. AM; art; free. Well-preserved Iron Age earth-house. Nearby is a fine late 16th-century doocot.

## Castles

**Ardblair Castle**  A923, 1 mile/1½ km west of Blairgowrie. By arrangement (tel. 0250 3155). 16th-century castle, home of the Oliphant family. Lady Nairne (*née* Oliphant), who wrote 'Charlie is My Darling', has relics here.

**Blair Castle**   Off A9 in Blair Atholl. Easter-Oct, Mon-Sat: 10.00-17.00; Sun: 14.00-17.00. Seat of the Duke of Atholl, chief of Clan Murray. Fine collections of furniture, portraits and Jacobite relics. The Duke is the last person in Britain permitted to have his own private army, the Atholl Highlanders. Extensive grounds with walks and caravan park. *D, P, R, T.*

**Burleigh Castle**   Off A911, 2 miles/3 km north-east of Kinross. AM; std; free. A 16th-century tower house, the seat of the Balfours of Burleigh. Key-keeper at farm opposite.

**Edzell Castle**   Off B966, 6 miles/10 km north of Brechin. AM; std, closed Tues pm and Thur pm. Impressive ruin of early 16th-century castle. Superb garden with flower 'sculptures' (see under Gardens, p. 150). *P, T, G.*

**Elcho Castle**   Minor road on south side of River Tay, 4 miles/6 km east of Perth. AM; std. Fortified house, once a seat of the Earls of Wemyss.

**Finavon Castle**   A94, 7½ miles/12 km south-west of Brechin. Art (call first at Doocot shop); free. Stronghold dating back to early 14th century, which partly collapsed in 18th century when undermined by a river. *P.* Finavon Doocot is nearby (see p. 150).

**Finlanrig Castle**   South side of Loch Tay near Killin (A85). Art; free. Former Breadalbane stronghold with a beheading pit, the only one left in Scotland.

**Glamis Castle**   A94, 5 miles/8 km south-west of Forfar. May-Sept, Sun-Fri: 13.00-17.00. Late 17th-century castle on site of much earlier building associated with Malcolm II and linked with Macbeth. Childhood home of HM The Queen Mother and birthplace of HRH Princess Margaret. Fine collections of china, tapestry and furniture – and a resident ghost! *D, P, R, T, G.*

**Huntingtower Castle**   A85, 3 miles/5 km west of Perth. AM; std. 15th-century fortified mansion, formerly known as Ruthven Castle.

**Kellie Castle**   Off A92, 2 miles/3 km south-west of Arbroath. Mar-Oct: 11.00-17.00. 16th-century tower house still used as a dwelling house. Gallery of works by Scottish artists.

**Loch Leven Castle**   On an island in Loch Leven near Kinross. AM. Apr-Sept, Mon-Sat: 09.30-19.00; Sun: 14.00-19.00. Access by ferry. 15th-century tower where Mary Queen of Scots was imprisoned for nearly a year.

**Castle Menzies** B846 near Weem, 1 mile/1½ km west of Aberfeldy. Apr-Sept, Mon-Sat: 10.30-17.00; Sun: 14.00-17.00. 16th-century Z-plan fortified tower house with carved dormers. Clan Menzies Museum included.

**Powrie Castle** Off A929, 3 miles/5 km north of Dundee. By arrangement (tel. 0382 456743). 16th-century tower house undergoing restoration.

## Country Parks

**Clatto** 2 miles/3 km north-west of Dundee (40 acres/16 ha). Small park centred on a reservoir, with beach and patches of woodland. Ranger service. Water sports, swimming, fishing, paths. *P, T.*

**Crombie** Off B961, 2 miles/3 km north-east of Newbigging (12 miles/19 km north-east of Dundee) (300 acres/123 ha). Largely woodland surrounding a loch. No water sports permitted. Fishing, path network. Ranger service. *P, T.*

**Forfar Loch** Off A94, western edge of Forfar (210 acres/85 ha). Loch and surrounds divided into three distinct areas. In the east there is a Leisure Centre; the northern sector focuses on sailing and canoeing; and the western part of the park is a quieter area, with the emphasis on wildlife and walking. *D, P, R, T.*

**Monikie** Off B961, 1 mile/1½ km north of Newbigging (2 miles/3 km south-west of Crombie, above) (185 acres/75 ha). Largely made up of three reservoirs, used for fishing and water sports, with some woodland. Ranger service. *P, T.*

## Gardens

**Abercairney** Off A85, 4½ miles/7 km east of Crieff. Apr-Sept, Wed only: 08.00-dusk. Extensive grounds with daffodils, rhododendrons, azaleas.

**Bolfracks** A827, 2 miles/3 km west of Aberfeldy. Mid-Apr-mid-Oct: 14.00-18.00. Shrubs, bulbs, alpines and perennials.

**Branklyn** South side of Perth on A85. Mar-Oct, daily: 10.00-dusk. Outstanding collection of plants especially alpines (NTS).

**Cluny House** 3½ miles/6 km from Aberfeldy, on Weem-Strathtay road. Mar-Oct, daily: 14.00-18.00. Woodland garden with specimen trees, shrubs, rhododendrons. Himalayan plant collection.

**Edzell Castle and Garden**  B966, 6 miles/10 km north of Brechin. AM; opening std, but closed Tues pm and Thur pm. Unique heraldic 'sculptures' in plants and shrubs, and flower-filled walled recesses make an outstanding formal garden. See also Edzell Castle (p. 148).

**Megginch Castle**  A85, 10 miles/16 km east of Perth. Apr-June and Sept, Wed only: 14.00-17.00; July-Aug, Mon-Fri: 14.00-17.00. In season, fine daffodils, rhododendrons, roses. Kitchen garden, ancient yews. House (15th century) not open.

## Historic Buildings and Monuments

**Black Watch Memorial**  B846, just north of Aberfeldy. Art; free. A large cairn topped by a kilted figure which commemorates the raising of the regiment in 1739. The famous General Wade's bridge is nearby.

**Dunkeld Little Houses**  In Dunkeld. Art (exterior only). A remarkable piece of restoration by NTS and Perthshire County Council of town houses dating from 1689. Not open to view, but NTS visitor centre open Easter-end May, Sept-Dec, Mon-Sat: 10.00-13.00, 14.00-16.30; June-Aug, Mon-Sat: 10.00-18.00; Sun: 14.00-17.00.

**Finavon Doocot**  Off A94, 7½ miles/12 km south-west of Brechin. Mid-May-Sept, daily: 13.00-17.00. The largest doocot in Scotland with over 2,000 nesting boxes. Exhibition. Finavon Castle is nearby (see p. 148).

**Hermitage**  Off A9, 2 miles/3 km west of Dunkeld. NTS; art. A 'folly' of 1758, set above the gorge of the River Braan. Walks in surrounding woods.

**Innerpeffray Library**  B8062, 4 miles/7 km south-east of Crieff. Open all year, Mon-Wed, Fri-Sat: 10.00-13.00, 14.00-16.00 (17.00 May-Sept); Sun: 14.00-16.00. Founded in 1691, this is the oldest library still in existence in Scotland. Early 16th-century church nearby.

**Melville Monument**  On Dunmore, 1 mile/1½ km north of Comrie. Art; free. Obelisk to the memory of Lord Melville (1742-1811), standing on hill with commanding views of surrounding countryside. Access by footpath, past Comrie House.

**Scone Palace**  A93, 2 miles/3 km north of Perth. Easter-mid-Oct, Mon-Sat: 10.00-17.30. 16th-century palace with later additions, all in grand style, now owned by the Earl of Mansfield. Site of early coronations using the famous Stone of Scone. Fine furniture, porcelain, old clocks. Extensive grounds with pinetum. *D, P, R, T, G.*

**Scott and Wilson Monument** Glen Prosen, 4 miles/7 km north of Kirriemuir. Art; free. A fountain erected to honour the Antarctic explorers who reached the South Pole in 1912.

## Industry

**Blair Atholl Mill** Off A9 in Blair Atholl. Apr-Oct, Mon-Sat: 10.00-18.00; Sun: 12.00-18.00. Milling of wheat and oats, and baking in working water mill. Shop and café selling mill produce. *P, R, T.*

**Glen Turret Distillery** Off A85, 1 mile/1½ km west of Crieff. Mar-Oct, Mon-Fri: 10.00-12.30, 13.30-16.00. Tours obligatory. Full process of distilling to produce malt whisky explained, plus tasting. *P, R, T.*

**Lighthouse** Montrose (Scurdie Ness) (tel. 0674 2655).

## Museums

**Alyth Museum** Commercial Street, Alyth (A93). May-Sept, Tue-Sat: 13.00-17.00. Museum of local life. Free.

**Angus Folk Museum** Kirkwynd Cottages, Glamis; 12 miles/20 km north of Dundee, off A94. May-Sept, daily: 12.00-17.00. Displays of domestic and farm implements and rural life (NTS).

**Crieff Museum** Lodge Street, Crieff. May-Sept, Tue-Sat: 13.00-17.00. Museum of local life and history. Free.

**Edzell Craft Museum** Dalhousie Street, Edzell; 6 miles/10 km north of Brechin on A94. Apr-Sept, daily: 10.00-18.00. Changing displays of local craft work and collection of geological interest. Free.

**Glenesk Folk Museum** Tarfside, Glenesk; 10 miles/16 km north-west of Edzell. Easter-May, Sun only: 14.00-18.00; June-Sept, daily: 14.00-18.00. Former shooting lodge containing displays of life in the area.

**Lighthouse Museum** Arbroath (tel. 0241 72609/76680).

**Museum of Scottish Tartans** In Comrie, on A85 Perth-Loch Earn road. Mid-Mar-end Oct, Mon-Sat: 09.00-17.00; Sun: 14.00-16.00; Nov-mid-Mar, Mon-Fri: 10.00-16.00; Sat: 10.00-13.00. Museum devoted to the history and development of tartans and Highland dress.

**Muthill Museum**   The Cross, Muthill; 3 miles/5 km south of Crieff, on A822. Easter week and June-Sept, Tue-Sat: 14.30-17.00. Displays of local life and history. Free (donations invited).

**Smiddy Museum**   Dunira Street, Comrie. Easter-Oct, Sat: 11.00-13.00, 14.30-16.30. Displays tools, forges and bellows from the blacksmith's trade. Free.

# Nature Reserves

**Ben Lawers** (NCC/NTS)   Visitor centre (Easter-Sept) on minor road from A827, 5 miles/8 km east of Killin to Glen Lyon. Nature trail, guided walks in summer, leaflets, warden. Further information locally or from NTS.

**Balgavies Loch** (SWT)   Car park on A932, 5 miles/8 km east of Forfar. Wintering wildfowl and wetland breeding birds. Hide available by arrangement with warden: Wielstaves Cottage, Letham, Forfar, Angus.

**Killiecrankie** (RSPB/NTS)   Famous Highland gorge and pass, scene of a battle in 1715. Escorted visiting Apr-Aug by arrangement with warden: Old Faskally Cottage, Killiecrankie (0796 3233 (centre) or 3245 (home). NTS visitor centre on A9 road.

**Loch Leven** (NCC)   The most important freshwater area in Britain for migratory and breeding wildfowl. Stopover point in autumn for thousands of geese. For visitor facilities see *Vane Farm*, below.

**Loch of Kinnordy** (RSPB)   Car park on B951, 1 mile/1½ km west of Kirriemuir. Hides open Apr-Aug, Wed and Sun: 10.00-17.00; Sept-Nov, Sun only: 10.00-17.00. Other times by arrangement with warden: The Flat, Kinnordy Home Farm, Kirriemuir DD8 5ER.

**Loch of Lintrathen** (SWT)   View from B951 road, 5 miles/8 km west of Kirriemuir. Hide available on open days, apply Hon. Warden: Freuchies, Glen Isla, by Kirriemuir, Angus.

**Loch of the Lowes** (SWT)   Visitor centre off A923, 2 miles/3 km east of Dunkeld. Advance booking necessary for groups. Warden at Loch of the Lowes Centre, by Dunkeld, Perthshire.

**Montrose Basin** (SWT)   Extensive tidal mudflats, inland from Montrose. Hide facilities by arrangement with warden: South Tillysole Cottage, Kinnaird Estate, by Brechin, Angus.

**Vane Farm** (Loch Leven) (RSPB)   Visitor centre on B9097, on south side of Loch Leven near Kinross. Open all year; Nov-Mar, weekends only: 10.00-16.30; Apr-Oct, daily, except Fri: 10.00-17.00. Many thousands of duck winter on the loch, and geese pass through in autumn.

# Religious Houses

**Restenneth Priory**   Off B9113, 1½ miles/2½ km east of Forfar. AM; art; free. Augustinian foundation from 12th century with tall square tower. There are also traces of a Saxon church dating from AD 710.

**St Bean's Church**   Fowlis Wester, off A85, 5 miles/8 km east of Crieff. Art; free. Attractive 13th-century church with carved Pictish stone cross.

**St Mary's Church Grandtully**   Pitcairn Farm, off A827, 2 miles/3 km east of Aberfeldy. AM; art; free. 16th-century church with fine painted wood ceiling featuring heraldic subjects.

**Tullibardine Chapel**   Off A823, 8 miles/13 km south-east of Crieff. AM; art; free (apply to farm nearby). Collegiate church founded mid-15th century and still largely unaltered.

# Visitor Centres

**Ben Lawers Visitor Centre**   Off A827, 6 miles/10 km east of Killin via mountain road. Mid-Apr-Sept, daily: 11.00-16.00 (June-Aug: 10.00-17.00). Sited at 1,300 feet (400 m), the centre has displays on the rare flora to be found on Perthshire's highest mountain and information on terrain and wildlife. Ranger service. Nature trail, guided walks (NTS).

**Glenruthven Weaving Mill and Heritage Centre**   Off A9 in Abbey Road, Auchterarder. May-Sept, Sat-Sun: 09.00-17.00. New centre with the only working steam textile engine in Scotland and other displays.

**Killiecrankie**   A9, 2½ miles/4 km north of Pitlochry. Easter-June and Sept-Oct, daily: 10.00-18.00; July-Aug, daily: 09.30-18.00. Exhibition of Battle of Killiecrankie (1689), natural history of area, walks, ranger service, tourist information (NTS).

**Tummel Forest Centre**   B8019, 5½ miles/9 km north-west of Pitlochry. Easter-Sept, Mon-Sat: 09.30-17.30; Sun: 10.00-17.30. Local history and industries on display, audio-visual programme, forest walks, reconstructed 'clachan' and ring fort. Free.

**Glengoulandie Deer Park** B846, 9 miles/15 km north of Aberfeldy. All year, daily: 09.00-one hour before sunset. Red deer and other native species in a natural setting.

## Forest Walks

**Allean** Tummel Forest. ¼ mile/½ km west of Queen's View on B8019, 5 miles/8 km north-east of Pitlochry. Short forest walk, excavated ring fort, reconstructed clachan. *P, T (D)*.

**Faskally** A9, 1 mile/1½ km north of Pitlochry. Three walks (1½ miles/2½ km, 2½ miles/4 km, 4 miles/7 km). Information centre open Apr-Sept. *P, G, T*.

**Hermitage Forest Trail** B898, 2 miles/3 km west of Dunkeld (NTS). Woodland trail by the River Braan, waterfalls, and passing the Hermitage (see p. 150), a picturesque 'folly' built in 1758 (1½ miles/2½ km). *P, G*.

**Kinnoull Hill Trail** Off A85, on east edge of Perth. Woodland walk of 2½ miles/4 km, with information markers and fine views over River Tay. *P, G*.

**Queen's View** B8091, 5 miles/8 km north-west of Pitlochry. Short forest walk, visitor centre in summer months. *P, G, T (D)*.

**Rannoch Forest** Carie, 3 miles/5 km west of Kinloch Rannoch (B8019), on south Loch Rannoch road. Three associated walks of up to 6 miles/9 km with fine views. *P, T*.

## Nature Trails and Other Walks

**Arbroath Cliffs** Start from east end of Esplanade, Arbroath. Cliff trail of 3 miles/4½ km. *P, G* (from Arbroath tourist information centre).

**Crieff Nature Trail** Culcrieff Farm, off A85, north-west of Crieff (1½ miles/2½ km). Information from Crieff tourist information centre. *P, G*.

**Kindrogan Hill Trail** Kindrogan Field Centre, A924 from Bridge of Cally to Enochdhu, 8 miles/13 km east of Pitlochry. Hill path through forest and moorland. *P, G*.

**Linn of Tummel Trails** A9/B8079, 3 miles/5 km west of Pitlochry (NTS). Two walks (1¼ miles/2 km or 2½ miles/4 km). Information Centre, Killiecrankie (1 mile/1½ km to north), open Easter-Sept. *P, T, G* (at Killiecrankie).

# WESTERN ISLES

## Antiquities

**Callanish**  Off A858, 16 miles/25 km west of Stornoway, Isle of Lewis. AM; art; free. The second most important megalithic site in Britain after Stonehenge, probably raised 2000-1500 BC. An avenue of 19 monoliths leads to an impressive circle of 13 stones, with stone rows leading out in several directions.

**Dun Carloway**  Off A858, 15 miles/24 km north-west of Stornoway. AM; std; free. Splendid Iron Age broch still 30 feet/9 m high in places. *P.*

**Trushel Stone**  ½ mile/1 km north of A857 at Ballantrushel, Isle of Lewis. Art; free. Possibly the tallest monolith in Scotland, 20 feet/6 m high. Other stones nearby.

## Castles

**Kisimul Castle**  On an island off Castlebay, Barra. May-Sept, Wed and Sat pm only. Island stronghold of the MacNeils of Barra, noted pirates. Main tower is 12th century. The castle was restored recently by the 45th clan chief, an American architect.

## Gardens

**Lewis Castle**  West of the Harbour, Stornoway. Art; free. The castle and grounds were given to the people of Stornoway by Lord Leverhulme. The castle is used as a technical college, but the wooded grounds with fine displays of rhododendrons are open to all.

## Historic Buildings and Monuments

**Lewis Black House**  A858 at Arnol, 15 miles/24 km north-west of Stornoway. AM; std; closed Sun. Traditional Hebridean dwelling with central peat fire (no chimney) and thatched roof. Many of the original furnishings are displayed.

*A 'cleitt' or black house on Hirta, St Kilda*

**Flora MacDonald's Birthplace**  Off A865, ½ mile/1 km north of Milton, South Uist. Art; free. Cairn marking the place where Flora MacDonald, who assisted Prince Charles Edward Stuart in his escape to Skye, was born in 1722.

## Industry

**Hebridean Perfume Co.**  Tangusdale, A888, 1½ miles/2½ km west of Castlebay, Barra. Open all year, Mon-Fri: 09.00-17.00. Display of perfume-making, bottling and packaging. *D, P, R, T.*

**Lighthouses**  Tiumpan Head, Lewis (tel. 085187 201), Butt of Lewis (tel. 085181 201).

**Tong Studio**  B895, 3 miles/5 km north of Stornoway, Lewis. Jan-June and Sept-Dec, Mon-Fri: 18.00-22.00; Sat: 10.00-17.00; July-Aug, Mon-Sat: 10.00-17.00. Visitors can see artists recording on disc and tape, and cassette copying. Prior notice preferred (tel. 0851 4632).

## Museums

**Shawbost Museum**  A858, Shawbost, Isle of Lewis. Apr-Nov, Mon-Sat: 10.00-18.00. Display compiled by local school of items relating to crofting, fishing and domestic life. Free (donations invited).

**South Uist Folk Museum**  Bualadhubh, Eochar. May-Sept, Mon-Sat: 10.00-17.00. Traditional Outer Hebridean thatched cottage with furnishings and weaving loom.

## Nature Reserves

**Balranald** (RSPB)  Warden, Apr-Sept, at Goular, North Uist. Turn off A865 at Bayhead (signposted to Hougharry).

**Loch Druidibeg** (NCC)  North end of South Uist, off A865. Open all year, daily; free. The most important surviving breeding ground of the native greylag goose in Britain, in an environment of lochs and machair. Warden.

# Religious Houses

**Church of St Moluag**  Off A857, north end of Lewis. To visit, apply to McLeod's in Eoropie. Chapel probably dating from 12th century, restored and used for worship every Sunday.

**Cille Barra**  Eoligarry, north Barra. Art; free. Ruined church of St Barr, who gave his name to the island; part of a later monastery. Chapel of St Mary nearby.

**Our Lady of the Isles**  Reuval Hill, South Uist. Art; free. Statue of the Madonna and Child, 30 feet/9m high, by Hew Lorimer, erected in 1957 by the Catholic community.

**Our Lady of the Sorrows**  Garrynamonie, South Uist. Open all year, daily: 09.00-19.00; free. Modern church (1964), with mosaic on the front of the building depicting Our Lady of the Sorrows.

**St Clement's Church**  A859 Rodel, south end of Harris. AM; art; free. Cruciform church of early 16th century, richly decorated with carved stone slabs.

**Teampull na Trionaid**  Off A865, 8 miles/13 km south-west of Lochmaddy, North Uist. Ruins of a college and monastery founded in early 13th century. Other ancient monuments nearby.

**Ui Church**  Aignish, off A866, 2 miles/3 km east of Stornoway. Art; free. Ruined church with carved tombs of MacLeod chiefs.

# ORKNEY

## Antiquities

*Mainland*

**Brough of Birsay** Extensive remains of Norse houses and church on small island off north-west top of Mainland (tidal access). Std (closed Mon in winter); check tide times before going! Charge.

**Cuween Hill** ¾ mile/1¼ km south-east of Finstown. Std (key at farm); free. Megalithic passage tomb.

**Grain Earth-House** A965, ½ mile/¾ km north of Kirkwall Harbour. Std; free. Iron Age earth-house with stair leading to underground chambers.

**Gurness Broch** ½ mile/1 km north-east of Evie pier on east coast. Std; free. Iron Age broch still up to 10 feet/3 m high within a deep ditch.

**Maes Howe** Off A965, 10 miles/16 km west of Kirkwall. AM; std; charge. Huge burial mound with one of the finest chambers in Europe. Runic wall inscriptions made by Vikings.

**Rennibister Earth-House** A965, 4½ miles/7½ km north-west of Kirkwall. AM; std; free. Earth-house in a modern farmyard, a good example of its kind.

**Ring of Brodgar** Between Harray and Stenness Lochs, 5 miles/8 km north-east of Stromness. AM; art; free. Henge monument and stone circle with 36 of the original 60 stones remaining.

**Skara Brae** Skaill Bay, 6 miles/10 km north of Stromness. AM; std; charge. Neolithic village of *c.* 2500 BC, with ten houses containing stone beds, fireplaces and cupboards – a truly remarkable site. *P.*

**Stones of Stenness** On southern shore of Loch Harray, to east of B9055. Art; free. Henge with stone circle and central square of slabs.

**Unstan Chambered Tomb** A965, 2½ miles/4 km north-east of Stromness. AM; std; free. Large chambered tomb 6 feet/2 m high.

*Skara Brae, a neolithic village in Orkney*

**Wideford Hill**  On western side of the hill, 2½ miles/4 km west of Kirkwall. AM; std; free. Small chambered cairn accessible by trapdoor and ladder.

*Other Islands*

**Blackhammer**  On south coast of Rousay, north of the B9064. AM; art; free. Chambered tomb covered by a modern concrete roof.

**Cubbie Roo's Castle**  Island of Wyre. AM; std; free. Remains of Norse castle built by Kolbein Hruga in 12th century.

**Dwarfie Stane**  At HY 243004, in valley between Quoys and Rackwick, Hoy. AM; art; free. Large sandstone block with cell carved out.

**Holm Chambered Tomb**  On small island of Holm, off Papa Westray. AM; art; free. Chambered tomb with decorated stones.

**Knap of Howar**  Neolithic settlement on west coast of Papa Westray, with remains of two stone houses. AM; art; free.

**Knowe of Yarso**  On south coast of Rousay, at HY 405280. AM; art; free. Chambered tomb with three compartments.

**Midhowe**  On west coast of Rousay. AM; art; free. Chambered tomb now covered to protect the stonework and a broch 13 feet/4 m high and with outer buildings and ditch, fine location on a promontory.

**Quoyness**  On Els Ness peninsula, on south coast of Sanday. AM; std; free. Spectacular chambered tomb with main chamber 14 feet/4½ m high.

**Taversoe Tuick**  On south coast of Rousay, at HY 526276. AM; art; free. Two-storey chambered tomb.


# Castles

**Cubbie Roo's Castle**  See Antiquities section above.

**Noltland Castle**  Isle of Westray. AM; std; free. Extensive remains of 15th-century stronghold, built by the then Governor of Orkney, Thomas de Tulloch. Hall, vaulted kitchen and winding staircase still largely complete.

# Historic Buildings and Monuments

**Earl Patrick's Palace and Bishop's Palace**  Kirkwall. AM; std. Earl Patrick's Palace, dating from 1607, has been described as 'the most accomplished piece of Renaissance architecture left in Scotland'. Nearby is the Bishop's Palace, dating from the 14th century, with later additions.

**Earl's Palace, Birsay**  North end of Mainland, 11 miles/18 km north of Stromness. AM; art; free. Extensive remains of a 16th-century palace built for the Earls of Orkney.

**Kitchener Memorial**  Marwick Head, south-west of Birsay Bay. Art; free. Marks the place where the cruiser HMS *Hampshire*, with Lord Kitchener on board, was sunk in 1916.

**Martello Tower**  Defensive fort built during the invasion scare of the Napoleonic Wars and renovated for later use in the First World War. Art; free (exterior only).

# Industry

**Click Mill**  Off B9057, 2 miles/3 km north-east of Dounby. AM; art; free. Horizontal water mill still in working order.

**Highland Park Distillery**  1 mile/1½ km south of Kirkwall, on road signposted St Mary's Holm. Sep-June, Mon-Fri: 10.30 and 15.00. Tours obligatory. Full process of malt whisky production from malting to bottling. *P, T.*

**Orkney Chairs**  14 Palace Road, Kirkwall, Visits by arrangement (tel. 0856 2429). Manufacture of traditional Orkney chairs.

**Scapa Distillery**  Off A964, 2 miles/3 km south of Kirkwall. Feb-June and Aug-Nov, Wed and Thur: 14.00 by prior arrangement (tel. 0856 2071). Free. Brewing and distillation of malt whisky.

# Museums

**Corrigall Folk Museum**  Harray, 2 miles/3 km east of Dounby. Apr-Sept, Mon-Sat: 10.30-13.00 and 14.00-17.00; Sun: 14.00-19.00. Buildings and artefacts of a 19th-century Orcadian farm. Free.

**Norwood Antiques**  Graemeshall, Holm. May-Sept, Sun, Wed and Thur: 14.00-17.00 and 18.00-20.00. Examples of lustre ware, silver, glass, rare clocks and watches.

**Orkney Wireless Museum**  St Margaret's Hope, South Ronaldsay. Apr-Sept, Daily: 10.00-20.00. Museum of wartime communications equipment and old domestic wireless sets.

**Stromness Museum**  52 Alfred Street, Stromness. Open all year, except public holidays and most of Feb, Mon-Sat: 11.00-12.30 and 13.30-17.00 (not Thur pm). Excellent natural history collection and exhibits on fishing, whaling and boat-building, and related to the Scapa Flow incidents in the First World War.

**Tankerness House Museum**  Broad Street, Kirkwall. Open all year except public holidays, Mon-Sat: 10.30-12.30 and 13.30-17.00. Tells the story of the islands over 5,000 years.

## Nature Reserves

**Copinsay** (RSPB)  Island reserve, access by boat from Skaill (tel. 085674 252) or from Newark Bay (tel. 085674 245).

**Dale of Cottasgarth** (RSPB)  Access at all times from car park at Lower Cottasgarth; turn left from A966, 3 miles/5 km north of Finstown.

**Hobbister** (RSPB)  4 miles/7 km from Kirkwall. Access at all times to land between A964 and the sea only.

**Marwick Head** (RSPB)  Access at all times from path northwards from Marwick Bay; leave cars at road end. No warden.

**North Hill, Papa Westray** (RSPB)  Summer warden (May-July) c/o Gowrie, Papa Westray, Orkney KW17 2BU. Entrance at north end of island's main road.

**Noup Cliffs, Westray** (RSPB)  Minor road from Pierowall to Noup Farm, then track to lighthouse. No warden.

## Religious Houses

**Italian Chapel**  St Margaret's Hope, Lamb Holm, South Ronaldsay. Art; free. A wartime Nissen hut converted into a chapel by Italian prisoners of

*The Italian Chapel, South Ronaldsay, Orkney*

war, using scrap metal and other available material to produce a strangely beautiful effect.

**Orphir Church**  A964, 6 miles/10 km south-west of Kirkwall. AM; art; free. Remains of the only circular medieval church in Scotland, built in the 12th century.

**St Magnus Cathedral**  Kirkwall. Open all year, Mon-Sat: 09.00-13.00 and 14.00-17.00. Free. 12th-century foundation, with additions up to 15th century. Still in regular use, it contains some of the finest examples of Norman architecture anywhere in Scotland. The dedicatee, Saint Magnus, is buried here.

**St Magnus Church**  Isle of Eglisay. AM; art; free. Impressive remains of 12th-century church with remarkable 'Irish' style round tower.

**Westside Church**  Tuquoy, south coast of Westray. AM; art; free. Remains of 12th-century church, with chancel which was later lengthened.

# SHETLAND

## Antiquities

**Clickhimin**  ¾ mile/1¼ km south-west of Lerwick. AM; std; free. Iron Age broch on site of earlier fort. Walls still 17 feet/5 m high.

**Mousa**  Island off Sandwick, 14 miles/22 km south of Lerwick. AM. The best preserved of all the island brochs, with walls still over 40 feet/13 m high. Access by boat from Sandwick.

**Ness of Burgi**  At south end of Mainland, 1 mile/1½ km south-west of Jarlshof. AM; art; free. Defensive Iron Age structure related to the brochs.

**Staneydale**  At HU 285503, 3 miles/4½ km north-east of Walls. AM; art; free. Second millennium BC 'temple' with oval internal chamber.

## Castles

**Muness Castle**  South-east point of Isle of Unst. AM; std; free. Late 16th-century building still in good condition, with many points of fine architectural detail.

**Scalloway Castle**  A6073, 5 miles/8 km west of Lerwick. AM; std; free. Substantial remains of early 17th-century castle built by Earl Patrick Stewart and abandoned after his death in 1615.

## Historic Buildings and Monuments

**Croft House**  Dunrossness, east of A970 at south end of Mainland, 25 miles/40 km south of Lerwick. May-Sept, Tue-Sun: 10.00-13.00 and 14.00-17.00. A croft complex with 19th-century house, restored and with all authentic furniture.

**Fort Charlotte**  Lerwick. AM; std; free. Mid-17th-century defensive fort built to protect the Sound of Bressay. Burned in 1673, it was restored in 1780.

**Jarlshof** Sumburgh Head, south end of Mainland. AM; std, but closed Tue pm, Wed pm. Remarkable archaeological site with traces of three settlements dating from Bronze Age to Viking times, a medieval farm, and a house built in 16th century by the Earls Stewart.

## Industry

**Hjaltasteyn** Whiteness, 9 miles/15 km west of Lerwick. All year, Mon-Fri: 09.30-13.00, 14.00-17.00. Free. Stone polishing workshop making gemstones.

**Shetland Workshop Gallery** Burns Lane, Lerwick. Open all year, Thur-Tue; 09.30-13.00 and 14.15-17.00. Two former dwelling houses in the old part of Lerwick converted to serve as a workshop and gallery for local artists and craftsmen.

## Museums

**Shetland Museum** Lower Hillhead, Lerwick. Open all year; opening times vary – enquire locally; closed Sun. Tells the story of man in the islands over 5,000 years, with sections devoted to art, textiles, ships, etc.

**Tingwall Valley** Veensgarth, off A971, 5 miles/8 km north-west of Lerwick. May-Sept, Tue, Thur and Sat: 10.00-13.00 and 14.00-17.00. Private collection of crofting tools and equipment housed in an 18th-century granary, stables and bothy.

## Nature Reserves

**Fetlar** (RSPB) Island reserve famous for its snowy owls, their only nesting site in the British Isles. Access to bird sanctuary only by arrangement with summer warden: Bealance, Fetlar ZE2 9DJ (tel. 095783 246).

**Lumbister, Mid Yell** (RSPB) Moorland site, west of A968 road. Access by arrangement with summer warden: Windhouse, Mid Yell, Shetland.

**Noss** (NCC) Island reserve, 4 miles/6 km east of Lerwick. Superb sandstone cliffs with large numbers of seabirds; important breeding colonies of great and arctic skua. Visitor centre, leaflet. Ferry across Noss Sound in summer.

# Religious Houses

**St Ninian's Isle** B9122, 20 miles/32 km south of Lerwick. Art; free. Remains of 12th-century chapel and Celtic church where a hoard of silver, now in the National Museum of Antiquities, Edinburgh, was discovered.

# APPENDIX—Who Does What

This appendix gives addresses and brief details on a number of bodies and organisations concerned with the Scottish countryside. Fuller details can be found in the booklet *Scotland's Countryside: Who's Who* (obtainable from the Countryside Commission for Scotland) or from the organisations themselves.

*Association for the Protection of Rural Scotland*

Secretary: Robert L. Smith, 14A Napier Road, Edinburgh EH10 5AY
APRS is a voluntary body concerned with the protection of the countryside, including country towns and villages, from unnecessary disfigurement and damage.

*British Association for Shooting and Conservation*

Scottish Office: Buchanan Home Farm, Drymen, by Glasgow G63 0BR
Founded in 1908 as the Wildfowlers' Association (WAGBI), the Association is Europe's largest representative body concerned with field sports. Scottish activities are concerned with the establishment of nature reserves with controlled shooting, the holding of country fairs with educational input, and political and environmental representation.

*British Deer Society*

Green Lane, Ufton Nervet, Reading, Berks RG7 4HA
The Society's aims are the study and the dissemination of knowledge of deer; the promotion of proper and humane methods of management, conservation and control of deer; and the provision of advice on all matters relating to deer. It is not a hunter's organisation, although the need for properly conducted control is fully recognised.

*Countryside Commission for Scotland*

Battleby House, Redgorton, Perth PH1 3EW
CCS is an official body set up under the Countryside (Scotland) Act of 1967 to advise the Secretary of State for Scotland and planning authorities on planning matters relating to the countryside. A wider explanation of its aims and work is given on page 41.

*Environmental Resource Centre*

Drummond High School, Cochran Terrace, Edinburgh EH7 4QP
ERC is an independent trust which functions as a project and resource base

170

for schools, youth and community groups in Lothian Region. Practical projects connected with nature conservation, environmental education and self-help community work are arranged.

## Forestry Commission

231 Corstorphine Road, Edinburgh EH12 7AT
The Commission manages over a million acres of commercial forest in Scotland. Many facilities for public recreation are provided, including waymarked walks, picnic and camp sites, and nature trails. The Commission's Information Branch will be pleased to supply further details (see also the section on page 24).

## Friends of the Earth (Scotland) Ltd

53 George IV Bridge, Edinburgh EH2 2JR
The Friends' aim internationally is the conservation, restoration and rational use of the environment and to this end it campaigns in Scotland on such issues as conservation of wildlife and wildlife habitat, better land use, control of pollution and the indiscriminate use of pesticides.

## Institute of Terrestrial Ecology

Bush Estate, Penicuik, Midlothian EH26 0QB *and*
Hill of Brathens, Glassel, Banchory, Kincardineshire AB3 4BY
The Institute of Terrestrial Ecology undertakes research on plant and animal populations and communities with the aim of improving the management and conservation of natural resources and predicting the consequences of management changes.

## Mountain Bothies Association

Secretary: Richard Genner, 42 Lamberton Court, Pencaitland, East Lothian
MBA is a charity whose aim is to prepare and maintain simple unlocked shelters in remote country for the use of all outdoor enthusiasts who love the wild and lonely places. Work parties to repair and maintain bothies are regularly arranged.

## Mountaineering Council of Scotland

Secretary: Chris Eatough, South Tillysole Cottage, Kinnaird Estate, by Brechin, Angus
The Mountaineering Council of Scotland was constituted in 1970 as the representative body of mountaineering clubs in Scotland. Its aims are to protect the ethos of mountaineering in Scotland; to protect the mountain environment from harmful development; to make known the views and interests of its members; and to co-operate with other organisations with common interests.

### National Farmers Union of Scotland

17 Grosvenor Crescent, Edinburgh EH12 5EN
The NFU is the voice of farming. It aims to watch over, protect and promote the interests of agriculture in all its branches and to encourage the development of the industry.

### National Trust for Scotland

5 Charlotte Square, Edinburgh EH2 4DU
NTS was formed in 1931 to 'promote the preservation of places of historic and architectural interest or of natural beauty'. Its properties range from castles to mountain ranges. Ranger services are provided at many properties and visitor centres furnish advice and information.

### Natural Environment Research Council

Northstar Avenue, Swindon, Wiltshire SN2 1EU
NERC has responsibility to encourage, plan and carry out research in those sciences which relate to man's natural environment and its resources. It funds fellowships and post-graduate studentships. In Scotland it also funds the Marine Research Laboratory at Dunstaffnage, near Oban; the Institute of Marine Biochemistry at Aberdeen; the Scottish office of the Institute of Geological Sciences; and the stations of the Institute of Terrestrial Ecology.

### Nature Conservancy Council

Scottish Headquarters: 12 Hope Terrace, Edinburgh EH9 2AS
The NCC advises the government on nature conservation policy and has a general duty to provide advice and disseminate information about nature conservation. It maintains and manages nearly 200 nature reserves in Britain, 60 of which are in Scotland. The NCC also notifies Sites of Special Scientific Interest (SSSIs) to planning authorities and grants or approves licences in connection with legislation protecting wildlife.

### Ramblers Association

Scottish Area: 3 Coats Place, Dundonald, Ayrshire KA2 9DJ
The RA's aims are to encourage rambling and mountaineering; to foster a greater knowledge, love and care of the countryside; and to work for the preservation of natural beauty, the protection of footpaths and the provision of access to open country.

### Red Deer Commission

Knowsley, 82 Fairfield Road, Inverness IV3 5LH
The Commission has a statutory responsibility for the conservation and control of red deer in Scotland. It is an independent body whose members are appointed by the Secretary of State for Scotland.

## Royal Scottish Forestry Society

1 Rothesay Terrace, Edinburgh EH3 7UP
The Society encourages the planting of trees and seeks to bring together, for their mutual benefit, those engaged in any way in the forestry industry in Scotland, and lovers of the Scottish countryside. It organises a full programme of meetings and excursions, and holds an annual conference.

## Royal Society for the Protection of Birds

Scottish Office: 17 Regent Terrace, Edinburgh EH7 5BN
RSPB is the largest voluntary wildlife conservation body in Europe. It manages over 30 reserves in Scotland, must of which can be visited by the public. Specialist staff can advise on such matters as oil pollution, planning, agriculture and forestry.

## Saltire Society

Saltire House, 13 Atholl Crescent, Edinburgh EH3 8HA
The Society is concerned with all aspects of the arts and the environment in Scotland. Among many other matters, it gives consideration to land renewal projects, historic buildings and gardens in the countryside, and pressures on 'wilderness areas'.

## Scottish Conservation Projects Trust

Scottish Office: 70 Main Street, Doune, Perthshire FK16 6BW
Voluntary organisation concerned with practical conservation work. Volunteers help to manage nature reserves and carry out a wide variety of tasks in towns and in the countryside. A range of specialist literature is available to help others with conservation work.

## Scottish Countryside Activities Council

Secretary: Dr Kathleen Watson, 39 Clepington Road, Dundee DD4 7EL
SCAC was formed in 1967. Its aims are to collect information relating to the use of the countryside for leisure activities; to spread knowledge about the countryside; to reconcile conflicting interests in its use; and to represent agreed interests to persons and authorities having responsibilities for the countryside. It acts therefore as an 'umbrella body' and a forum for countryside bodies to exchange views.

## Scottish Countryside Rangers Association

Secretary: Sue Manson, Ranger's Office, Hillend Park, Biggar Road, Edinburgh
SCRA aims to promote and encourage high standards of professionalism amongst countryside rangers in Scotland and to advise on matters relating to the structure, organisation and training of ranger services in Scotland.

## Scottish Field Studies Association

Kindrogan Field Centre, Enochdhu, Blairgowrie, Perthshire PH10 7PG
SFSA is an educational body which provides opportunities for people of all ages to expand their knowledge of countryside subjects. A wide range of courses is available for full-time students and interested amateurs.

## Scottish Landowners Federation

18 Abercromby Place, Edinburgh EH3 6TY
SLA aims to represent the owners of rural land in Scotland. Membership includes all sizes of ownership from large estates to small farms, and includes some local authorities. SLF supports responsible access to the countryside and tries to achieve co-operation between its members and those seeking recreational facilities in the countryside.

## Scottish Recreational Land Association

Haigh House, 18 Abercromby Place, Edinburgh EH3 6TY
The Association aims to encourage and assist owners and occupiers of land in Scotland to provide facilities for public recreation at the highest possible standards and on a sound, revenue-earning basis.

## Scottish Rights of Way Society Ltd

28 Rutland Square, Edinburgh EH1 2BW
The Society seeks to protect the public's interest in the preservation and maintenance of established rights of way in Scotland. It gives advice and help, and where necessary takes appropriate legal action. It also encourages the signposting of major rights of way.

## Scottish Sports Council

1 St Colme Street, Edinburgh EH3 6AA
The Council is a national agency responsible for encouraging the development of sport and physical recreation. It gives advice and encouragement for many outdoor sports, and operates three national sports training centres, two of which – Cumbrae in the Firth of Clyde and Glenmore Lodge in the Cairngorms – are concerned solely with outdoor activities.

## Scottish Tourist Board

23 Ravelston Terrace, Edinburgh EH4 3EU
The STB aims to attract visitors to Scotland, to co-ordinate the promotion of tourism in Scotland, and to encourage the development of visitor facilities and attractions. Board assistance has helped with countryside facilities such as holiday chalets, interpretive and visitor centres, and sporting facilities.

## Scottish Wild Land Group

St Ronan's, 93 Queen Street, Alva, Clackmannanshire FK12 5AH
The Group, formed only in 1982, aims to promote the conservation of wild land in Scotland by increasing public awareness of the problems facing such land and by pressing for the recognition of conservation as a relevant part of the national economy, compatible with the provision of employment, appropriate development, and the tourist industry, to which the landscape and its particular qualities are vital.

## Scottish Wildlife Trust

25 Johnston Terrace, Edinburgh EH1 2NH
SWT is a voluntary organisation which aims to promote better understanding of countryside problems through educational activities such as lectures and films, visitor centres and open days at reserves, practical conservation work and the establishment of nature trails and observation hides.

## PERTH AND KINROSS DISTRICT LIBRARY

This book is due for return on or before the last date indicated on label or transaction card. Renewals may be obtained on application. Loss of transaction cards will be charged at 10p. each.

Loss of Reader's tickets will be charged at 25p. for Plastic Type. 10p. for Manilla Type.

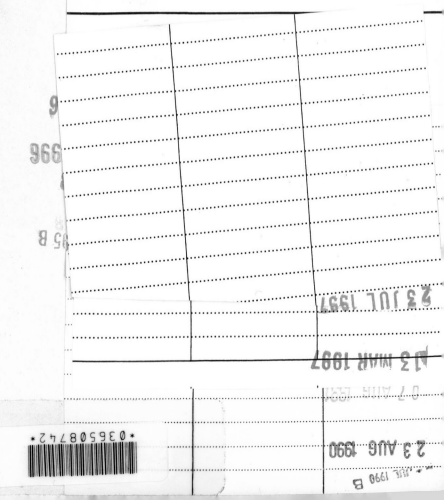